Licensed larceny

MANCHESTER
1824

Manchester University Press

The *Manchester Capitalism* book series

General Editor

MICHAEL MORAN

Manchester Capitalism is a series of short books which reframe the big issues of economic renewal, financial reform and political mobilisation. The books attack the limits of policy imagination in everything from university pedagogy to financial regulation. Our working assumption is that a reframing of policy choices is necessary before we can reform present-day capitalism.

Manchester Capitalism is also a group of researchers (www.manchestercapitalism.co.uk) whose work combines 'follow the money' research with political discussion of narrative alibis. Our distinctive analysis was pioneered in public interest reports about mundane activities like meat supply and railways for the Centre for Research on Socio-Cultural Change (www.cresc.ac.uk).

We write in the tradition of provincial radicalism for a broad audience of citizens because we believe there is much distributed intelligence in our society outside the metropolitan centres of elite decision making. Our work is politically challenging because it revives the liberal collectivism of Berle or Macmillan and borrows from free-thinking critics of capitalism like Wright Mills and Braudel.

The first two books in the series, *The End of the experiment? From competition to the foundational economy* and *What a waste: Outsourcing and how it goes wrong* both focused on the political economy of modern Britain. Nick Hildyard's new book adds a major study in the political economy of underdevelopment.

Licensed larceny

Infrastructure, financial extraction and the Global South

Nicholas Hildyard

Manchester University Press

Published by Manchester University Press
Altrincham Street, Manchester M1 7JA, UK
www.manchesteruniversitypress.co.uk

British Library Cataloguing-in-Publication Data
A catalogue record for this book is available from the British Library

Library of Congress Cataloging-in-Publication Data applied for

ISBN 978 1 7849 9427 3   paperback
ISBN 978 1 7849 9426 6   hardback

First published 2016

Typeset by Servis Filmsetting Ltd, Stockport, Cheshire
Printed in Great Britain by Bell and Bain Ltd, Glasgow

Contents

List of exhibits   vii
List of boxes   viii
Acknowledgements   ix
Abbreviations   xi

1 *Mise-en-scène*: the injustices of wealth   1
  1.1 Gattopardo politics   2
  1.2 Honouring capital's ghosts   4
  1.3 A road map for what is to follow   8
  Notes to Chapter 1   10

2 A study in financial extraction: Lesotho's national
  referral hospital   11
  2.1 The consortium   11
  2.2 The Public–Private Partnership deal   12
  2.3 Budgetary impacts   13
  2.4 Who takes the risks?   13
  2.5 Rates of return   16
  2.6 Who gets the profits?   17
  Notes to Chapter 2   20

3 Infrastructure as financial extraction   22
  3.1 Infrastructure through finance's eyes   22
  3.2 Guarantee me: piracy of the public by the private   25
  3.3 Public–Private Partnerships: bring on the
     (private) profits   29
  3.4 Stand and deliver   32
  3.5 Liens on the state   38
  Notes to Chapter 3   40

4 Extraction in motion: infrastructure-as-asset-class   41
    4.1 Yield hogs   41
    4.2 Extraction strategies and vehicles   43
    4.3 Fee factories   46
    4.4 Many happy returns (for the 1%)   47
    4.5 More guarantees, please   50
    Notes to Chapter 4   53

5 Infrastructure corridors, frontier finance and
  the vulnerabilities of capital   55
    5.1 Time, space and infrastructure   57
    5.2 Corridors, hubs and cities: a whistle-stop tour   61
    5.3 Frontier finance: whose cupboard is bare?   81
    Notes to Chapter 5   84

6 Reflections for activism   85
    6.1 The cry of injustice   88
    6.2 Friendship as 'the political tool of the moment'   92
    6.3 In support of impolite politics   95
    Notes to Chapter 6   99

References   100

List of exhibits

2.1   Who takes the risks?   16
2.2   Netcare's ten top shareholders in 2015   18
3.1   Major types of Public–Private Partnerships (PPPs)   30
4.1   Reported returns by infrastructure asset type
      and estimates of extraction   49
5.1   Development corridors in sub-Saharan Africa   66
5.2   IIRSA's ten 'Integration and Development Hubs'   69
5.3   Indonesia's MP3EI economic corridors   74
5.4   Transport corridors in the 'Greater Mekong subregion'   76
5.5   India's economic corridors   77
5.6   One Belt, One Road   80

List of boxes

1.1	Global looting – a snapshot	5
2.1	When public is private and private is public	14
2.2	Financial extraction? Netcare and Tsepong response	19
3.1	The violence of 'contracted income streams'	24
3.2	Infrastructure: how much is invested?	26
3.3	The economic metabolism of loans and guarantees – a word or two from Rosa Luxemburg	27
3.4	PPPs: pushing private profits	31
4.1	The global pensions grab	51
5.1	The Maputo Development Corridor	64
5.2	Corridors of violence	72
5.3	Made in the World @ World Trade Organization	79

Acknowledgements

This book reflects numerous conversations over several decades with colleagues around the world with whom I have worked to support those adversely affected by large-scale infrastructure projects and to understand the complexities of modern finance and accumulation. They are too numerous to mention by name, but I hope they know who they are. To them I owe special thanks for their friendships, their generosity of intellectual spirit, their critical analysis and their encouragement to keep probing.

The book's more immediate history started with a presentation I gave in July 2014 on the connections between Public–Private Partnerships, financial extraction and inequality to students studying with Karel Williams, Professor of Accounting and Political Economy at Manchester Business School. Karel subsequently invited me to develop the presentation into a book for the Manchester Capitalism series of Manchester University Press. I owe a particular thanks to him not only for his midwifery of this book, but also, and more so, for encouraging me to explore 'finance as an extractive industry', an approach that he and his colleagues at the Centre for Research on Socio-Cultural Change (CRESC) have pioneered.

Several colleagues – Nancy Alexander, Mareike Beck, Peter Bosshard, Andrew Bowman, Joanna Cabello, Premrudee Daoroung, Soumitra Ghosh, Anna Marriott, Roger Moody, Mick Moran, Winnie Overbeek, Hendro Sangkoyo, Estella Schmid, Mohamed Suliman, Antonio Tricarico, Monica Vargas, Wiert Wiertsema and Ivonne Yanez – gave generously of their time to comment on draft chapters. I am very grateful to them for their insights and challenges, and hope I have done them justice. The final text is, however, my sole responsibility.

Netcare Hospitals (Pty) Ltd, a South African private healthcare provider, gave comments and factual clarifications on the case study of Lesotho's national referral hospital; I thank the company for these and their time.

Cartographer Don Shewan turned complicated drawings into clear and concise maps; I am grateful to him for his skills and patience. I thank Manchester University Press for their support and forbearance throughout this project.

Finally, none of my work would be possible without the friendship, critical encouragement and support of Larry Lohmann and Sarah Sexton, my colleagues for over twenty years at The Corner House. My thinking, politics and activism would not be what they are without them. I owe them a very special debt of gratitude.

Abbreviations

ACCA	Association of Certified Chartered Accountants
ADB	Asian Development Bank
ADBI	Asian Development Bank Institute
ASEAN	Association of Southeast Asian Nations
BBO	buy–build–operate
BDO	build–develop–operate
BIT	Bilateral Investment Treaty
BLOT	build–lease–operate–transfer
BOO	build–own–operate
BOT	build–operate–transfer
BOOT	build–own–operate–transfer
BRIC	Brazil Russia India China
BROT	build–rent–own–transfer
BTO	build–transfer–operate
CDO	collaterised debt obligation
CDC	Commonwealth Development Corporation
CDS	credit default swap
COSIPLAN	Committee of the South American Infrastructure and Planning Council
CPAL	Consumers' Protection Association (Lesotho)
CRESC	Centre for Research on Socio-Cultural Change
DBSA	Development Bank of Southern Africa
DfID	Department for International Development
DMIC	Delhi–Mumbai Industrial Corridor
DMICDC	Delhi–Mumbai Industrial Corridor Development Corporation
DVRL	Lúrio River Valley Development Project
EIB	European Investment Bank
EID	Ejes de Integración y Desarrollo
EIU	Economist Intelligence Unit
ESSU	European Services Strategy Unit
ETF	Exchange Traded Funds

FEC	financial and economic equilibrium
GIF	Global Infrastructure Facility
ICSID	International Centre for Settlement of Investment Disputes
IEG	Internal Evaluation Group
IIRSA	Initiative for the Integration of Regional Infrastructure in South America
IFC	International Finance Corporation
IL&FS	Infrastructure Leasing & Financial Services Limited
IMF	International Monetary Fund
IPA	Indian Ports Association
LAPSSET	Lamu Port South Sudan Ethiopia
LAWR	Latin America Weekly Report
LDO	lease-develop-operate
LEE	Lesotho Economic Empowerment
LPI	Logistics Performance Index
MCLI	Maputo Corridor Logistics Initiative
MDC	Maputo Development Corridor
MERCOSUR	Mercado Común del Sur
MIC	middle-income country
MIG	Macquarie Infrastructure Group
MIGA	Multilateral Investment Guarantee Agency
MIP	Macquarie Infrastructure Partners
MP3EI	Masterplan for Acceleration and Expansion of Indonesia's Economic Development
MRG	Minimum Revenue Guarantee
NAFTA	North American Free Trade Area
NEPAD	New Partnership for Africa's Development
OBOR	One Belt, One Road
OECD	Organization for Economic Co-operation and Development
PEI	Private Equity International
PFI	Private Finance Initiative
PIDA	Programme for Infrastructure Development in Africa
PPA	Power Purchasing Agreement
PPP	Public–Private Partnership
S&P	Standard & Poor's
SDI	Spatial Development Initiative
SEZ	Special Economic Zones
SME-CSMI	School of Mining Engineering and Centre for Sustainability in Mining and Industry

UCU	University and College Union
UEUA	Uganda Electricity Users Association
UN	United Nations
UNASUR	Union of South American Nations
UNDP	UN Development Programme
UNESC	United Nations Economic and Social Council
UNICEF	United Nations Children's Fund
VCCSII	Vale Columbia Center on Sustainable International Investment
WEF	World Economic Forum
WTO	World Trade Organization

Chapter 1
Mise-en-scène: *the injustices of wealth*

> What thoughtful rich people call the problem of poverty, thoughtful poor
> people call with equal justice a problem of riches.
>
> (R.H. Tawney 1914)

The world is riven by social injustices, and there are numerous
individuals, groups, political parties and social movements whose
commitment and dedication to challenging what Chilean poet Pablo
Neruda (2004, p. 1) called 'organised social misery' is a constant
inspiration. But no challenge that lacks a grounded understanding
of how wealth is accumulated within society, and by whom, is ever
likely to make more than a marginal dent in the status quo. Nor
will it shift accumulation's lethal trajectory of oppression, dispossession, environmental degradation and life-robbing inequalities. At
best, it may slow the processes through which elites extract value
from society every minute of every day; at worst, it may unwittingly
further the concentration of political and economic power, margin-
alisation, exclusion and looting that such extraction entails.

The relative ease with which elites have deflected mounting popular
protest over the growing worldwide gulf between rich and poor, and
the injustices that this reflects, is illustrative. Protests by Occupy!
and other movements have forced acknowledgment of the problem
by just about everyone from President Obama to the corporate head
honchos who gather every year at the World Economic Forum.
The International Monetary Fund (IMF) and the Organization for
Economic Co-operation and Development (OECD), both bastions
of neoliberalism, have now similarly 'discovered' inequality as an
'issue'. Some policy changes have been made: both the IMF and the
OECD have jettisoned years of defending inequality as necessary
to economic growth and now argue that it poses a barrier. Long-
standing demands that taxes on the rich be slashed have also been
modified to endorse progressive taxation as an appropriate policy
response to inequality. So, too, the damaging impacts of inequality

on the fabric of society, scrupulously documented by academics such as Richard Wilkinson and Kate Pickett (2009), have now been acknowledged.

Three cheers for all that! Except that, even as the IMF sheds crocodile tears over the 'dark shadow' that inequality is casting over the global economy, it continues to impose austerity measures on Greece and other countries. Except that what counts as 'excessive inequality' keeps shifting in the wrong direction. (Today it is asked whether an average wage differential between CEOs and workers of 300:1 is acceptable, whereas as recently as the 1970s a ratio of 20:1 was considered out of line.)[1] Except that inequality is still viewed primarily as a problem of poverty and the poor rather than of riches and the rich, an explanation that conveniently deflects attention from the role that wealth creation plays in *creating* inequality (Dorling 2010; Sayer 2015). Except that the structural causes of inequality remain unexamined and unchallenged. Everything changes so that nothing changes.

1.1 Gattopardo politics

Dissembling and damage control are to be expected from the likes of the IMF, which, as architect and chief enforcer of structural adjustment, has form on inequality. But much of the noise around inequality emanating from the mainstream Left also amounts to what academics (and self-styled 'bourgeois radicals') Ewald Engelen and Karel Williams (2014, p. 1771) describe as 'guaranteed inaction', whereby 'society can recognise the problem of growing inequality without any prospect of effective redress'.

An emblematic case in point is the response of the left-leaning French economist Thomas Piketty, whose 600-page doorstopper of a book, entitled *Capital in the Twenty-First Century*, hit the bestseller lists in 2014. Largely based on research undertaken over the previous decade with his colleague, Emmanuel Saez, Piketty exhaustively documents the historical data on income inequalities in 20 countries, citing a blizzard of statistics to dismantle claims that capitalism spreads wealth rather than concentrates it.

Piketty observes that, since 1700, capital (a term he uses as a synonym for 'wealth') has typically shown a pre-tax return of 4–5 per cent a year – far higher than the average growth of the economy as a whole (*The Economist* 2014a). Piketty boils this down to what he calls 'the first fundamental law of capitalism': namely, that 'the private rate of return on capital (r) tends to be significantly higher for long periods of time than the rate of growth of income and output (g)'. So, if wealth grows at 5 per cent but the economy grows only at 1 per cent, the rich have gains of 4 per cent which they can use to make more wealth. The result, over time, is that the wealth of the rich just accumulates and accumulates. In the absence of wars (which destroy wealth) or major redistributive initiatives, those who have wealth therefore tend to get wealthier, generating ever greater inequality, which simply snowballs over time as the wealthy become 'more and more dominant over those who own nothing but their labour'. Or, as Piketty (2014, p. 571) puts it, 'The past devours the future.'

The direction of travel is thus towards a return of 'patrimonial capitalism' marked by 'terrifying' inequalities of wealth and income, where the rich are rich largely because they have inherited large fortunes. Piketty's suggested solution is an 80 per cent rate of taxation on incomes over \$1 million and the introduction of a global wealth tax (Hear! Hear!).

So far so good. Picketty's law (r > g) succinctly encapsulates what we knew or already suspected: namely, that capitalism is an engine that remorselessly generates inequality. But challenging this inequality requires digging deeper. What are the structures that enable the wealthy to get their wealth in the first place? And, critically, what enables them to hold on to it? Piketty unfortunately only skims the surface.

A case in point is his treatment of 'capital' as merely valued objects. Under this definition, the hunting spears of an Amazonian tribe or the shed in a suburban garden are considered to be no different from the shares in a joint stock company or options on a future oil contract (Kunkel 2014). But they clearly *are* different: they may all constitute forms of wealth but they do not all constitute forms of 'capital'. For 'capital' is not a 'thing': it is a process, a set of constantly evolving and contested social, economic and political relationships that enable money to be used to make more money. The spear is not capital when used to kill an animal for the family cooking pot, any more than money, land, houses and industrial plant and equipment are capital when they are used to satisfy human needs without making profits. Quite the opposite. In fact, when they are not being used productively as part of a process of accumulation, they are the very antithesis of capital.

Geographer David Harvey (2014) observes that Piketty's *Capital* is not really a book about capital at all. By treating capital as a 'thing', Piketty (in common with many others) leaves out all that is important if inequality is to be confronted: class, relations of production, the political and legal infrastructures that underpin accumulation, the daily finessing of patterns of wealth extraction, unequal exchange and, critically, the distribution of political and economic power. The engine of inequality remains unexamined and thus unchallenged.

Piketty also seems reluctant to probe what might constitute a plausible political strategy for confronting the rich and dismantling their 'constructed institutions' of extraction. He advocates talking truth to power as the means of achieving change, albeit gloomily admitting that his call for a wealth tax is unlikely to be put into practice as long as it is the rich that he is talking to. As Ewald Engelen and Karel Williams (2014, p. 1771) of the Centre for Research on Socio-Cultural Change (CRESC) remark, this 'political reticence' renders Piketty's approach less effective than it might otherwise be as a means of actually redressing inequality: 'The rich can sleep soundly in their beds with Professor Piketty on our bookshelves.'

1.2 Honouring capital's ghosts

Clearly there is a need to probe beyond Piketty's blizzard of statistics. Such figures certainly provide a rough and ready measure of the extent to which elites have constructed institutions that extract value from society, and of the operational efficiency of such extractive institutions (see Box 1.1 'Global looting – a snapshot'). But without a deeper analysis of how value is created, the figures have little or no explanatory power and thus offer little in the way of action that would pose an effective challenge to inequality. Knowing that 1.5 million people in the US, the richest country in the world, and a billion more in the rest of the world live on less than $2 a day while Bill Gates, co-founder of Microsoft and (for the past sixteen years) the world's richest man, rakes in $140 a second (Live-Counter 2015) without having to lift a finger is a cause for anger: but it tells us little or nothing about the processes that enable Gates and other billionaires to accumulate their wealth or the relationship between those processes and the poverty of others. Indeed, without an analysis that places accumulation at its centre, inequality statistics can serve as a wake-up call to some but do not themselves challenge the growing gulf between the haves and the have-nots. Even calls for progressive taxation (a no-brainer as a tool for disempowering the rich, but only a limited tool) arguably threaten to become a regressive end-of-pipe 'solution' that perpetuates the violence of capital while retrospectively compensating a few of those from whom capital has looted, mainly in those richer countries where the wealth extracted historically from around the globe is currently concentrated.

Box 1.1 Global looting – a snapshot

In country after country, the incomes of the rich are skyrocketing, while those of poorer people stagnate or plummet; and the lion's share of global wealth is increasingly concentrated in fewer and fewer hands. Mainstream economists insist that inequality is simply one of the growing pains of economic development. The message is 'Be patient, a rising tide will lift all boats'.

For those billions of people who don't have a boat, such talk is cruelly cynical nonsense. Trickle down is not working – and never has. Instead of trickling down to irrigate all of society, wealth is gushing up, concentrating in the hands of the few.

Numerous reports now document the statistics of the global wealth gap. Although such data reveals little (and disguises much) about the social processes through which wealth is accumulated by the few, it does provide a snapshot of how effectively elites have, in the words of journalist Will Hutton, 'constructed institutions that extract value from the rest of society'. It is through that lens that the data is best viewed.

The figures for income tell a dismal story. In 1992 the UN Development Programme (UNDP) produced a diagram depicting how just over 80 per cent of total world income went to the top fifth of the world's people, while the bottom fifth got a paltry 1.5 per cent. The resulting 'champagne glass' image became a symbol of the vast gap between rich and poor. In 2007 researchers at the United Nations Children's Fund (UNICEF) revisited the figures and found that the percentages had barely shifted, despite global economic output doubling in the intervening years. The UNICEF researchers concluded that 'it would take more than eight centuries (855 years to be exact) for the bottom billion to have ten percent of global income'. Warren Buffett, one of the world's richest men (the vast majority of the world's super-rich are men and white) is candid: 'There's class warfare, all right, but it's my class, the rich class, that's making war, and we're winning.'

And income is only part of the inequality story. In many countries, inequalities in accumulated wealth are even wider than those in income, and they are growing. Oxfam calculates that, in 2013, just 85 people – the number of people you could get into just one London double-decker bus – controlled as much wealth as the bottom half of the world's adult population. A year later, the same amount of wealth was controlled by just 67 people.

The wealth gap between the richest and poorest countries is also growing. During the colonial period from 1820 to 1911, the income gap between the richest countries and the poorest countries widened from 3:1 to 11:1. By 1950, at a time when many countries were achieving independence, it was 35:1. Post-independence, the gap has not narrowed but increased: in 1999 the United Nations Development Programme estimated it was 79:1.

Looting is the only word for this process.

Source: Hildyard 2015

To give inequality numbers any meaning requires uncovering, understanding, exposing and organising against the many-stranded forms of wealth extraction that are invisible in graphs and computer models. The 'shining pin on which … billionaires pirouette' (to use the image of Booker Prize-winning Indian novelist and activist Arundhati Roy (2014)) is a product of thousands of everyday acts of exploitation of humans and non-humans, and of resistance to them. As Roy records, even the merely relatively rich who make up the new middle class of India

> live side by side with spirits of the netherworld, the poltergeists of dead rivers, dry wells, bald mountains, and denuded forests; the ghosts of 250,000 debt-ridden farmers who have killed themselves, and the 800 million who have been impoverished and dispossessed to make way for us.
>
> (Roy 2014, p. 12)

These 'ghosts of capitalism' are to be found wherever relationships are being forged that enable accumulation. They haunt the shiny new factories of China's free trade zones where low-waged workers produce iPads to make Apple's shareholders rich (Froud *et al.* 2012). Their blood inks the international free trade agreements – from NAFTA (Brennan 2015) to the proposed US–EU Transatlantic Trade and Investment Partnership (Hilary 2014) – that strip away labour rights and environmental controls, drive down wages and massively concentrate and enhance corporate power. They stalk the offices of the accountancy firms that pore over tax laws to find loopholes for their corporate clients (Sikka 2012). They lurk within the trillions of dollars of derivatives contracts that magic money out of money (Hildyard 2008). They are present everywhere in the myriad, interconnected processes of enclosure, dismantling, reconstruction, abstraction, quantification, monetisation and commodification that, historically and in the future, make it possible to appropriate the unpaid work of both non-humans and humans (Lohmann 2015). Much work has been done over the years by academics and activists to honour the lives of these ever-present spectres by illuminating the broad processes of wealth extraction that are responsible for their impoverishment, dispossession, exploitation and demise. As Karl Marx (2010) scrupulously documented over a century ago, wealth is extracted upwards because capitalists pay workers for only a fraction of the value they create through their labour – and snaffle the rest. Other means of extraction include rent and interest. These forms of looting – aka 'capitalism' – are now the institutionalised order in most countries around the world.

It takes hard political work to build the social, legal and economic infrastructure that embeds such forms of extraction to the point where they are assumed to be 'normal'. As long as capital expands, that hard work is never done. Labour must not only be commodified where it is not commodified, but new ways must be found to squeeze more profit from it; previously unexploited forms of social solidarity must be transformed into a form that can yield profit; existing markets must be nurtured and new markets created; old forms of rent expanded and new income streams created from which rents can be extracted; property rights upheld and established in areas where property has not previously been recognised; and so on. A constantly watchful eye is therefore essential if these new forms of financial extraction are to be blocked, short-circuited, deflected or unsettled.

So when the World Bank, the G20 group of nations, the World Economic Forum, the OECD and other well-known enablers of wealth extraction start to organise to promote greater private-sector involvement in 'infrastructure', with plans to spend $50–70 trillion over the next fifteen years on programmes aimed at expanding capital, activists' alarm bells should begin to ring. How are roads, bridges, hospitals, ports and railways being eyed up by finance? What bevels and polishes the lens through which they are viewed? How is infrastructure being transformed into 'assets' that will yield the returns now demanded by investors? How much wealth is already being extracted by finance from infrastructure? And how? What role do Public–Private Partnerships (PPPs), now being pushed throughout the global South as the 'solution' to a claimed infrastructure funding deficit, play in the extraction process? And why now? What does the reconfiguration of infrastructure tell us about the vulnerabilities of capital?

The challenge is not only to understand the mechanisms through which infrastructure is being reconfigured to extract wealth: equally important is to think through how activists might best respond. Policy change is clearly critical, but policy proposals without a plausible political strategy for confronting institutionalised wealth extraction (of which 'infrastructure' is only one example) have little purchase if they are not part of a deeper, critical assessment of why elites are able to get away with accumulation. Is activists' work inadequate only because activists don't shout loudly enough against iniquities, or produce enough bullet-pointed reports outlining proposals for change? Or are there also perhaps more promising ways of building or strengthening ways of living that respect the collective right of all (not just the few) to decent livelihoods? What oppositional strategies genuinely unsettle elite power instead of making it stronger?

1.3 A road map for what is to follow

These and other questions weave their way through this book. Its immediate focus is infrastructure, but the book is also intended as a modest, practical contribution to encouraging both wider understanding of the evolving institutional means through which elites accumulate wealth at society's expense and more critical reflection on ways of organising against capital. Here is a road map to the rest of the book:

Chapter 2 starts with a concrete example of infrastructure-as-extraction – a detailed case study of Lesotho's Queen 'Mamohato Memorial Hospital, built and operated by a private sector consortium under a Public–Private Partnership (PPP) contract. The chapter traces the flows of money into and out of the project – and highlights who benefits from them. It argues that the PPP arrangement clearly serves to extract considerable wealth from one of the poorest countries in the world and siphon part of it to the elite 1% of the global rich. And, before any lawyers start typing out libel writs, let it be emphasised that there is no suggestion of any dodgy dealing here. On the contrary: the central concern is that the extraction is entirely lawful.

Chapter 3 builds on the Lesotho example to explore how finance views infrastructure and the ways in which infrastructure is being reworked to provide what finance seeks of it: stable, contracted income streams. One focus is on the contractual arrangements that investors are putting in place through Public–Private Partnerships to ensure guaranteed (yes, guaranteed) high rates of profit. Even though the state remains the major financier and operator of public services, the relatively small space that has now been opened up for private investors has enabled finance to construct a multi-billion-dollar extraction machine, with major ramifications for inequality.

Chapter 4 looks beyond PPPs at other investment vehicles that are being used or developed to extract wealth, directly or indirectly, from the activities that surround the funding, construction and operation of infrastructure – and attempts to quantify the amount of money now being extracted. The trajectory is not only towards increased inequality: it is also profoundly undemocratic, elitist and unstable. Undemocratic because a handful of fund managers now increasingly determine what gets financed and what does not. Elitist because the facilities that would most benefit the poor do not get built. And unstable because infrastructure-as-asset-class is a bubble that is set to burst.

Chapter 5 seeks to understand the structural forces behind the emergence of infrastructure-as-asset-class and the vulnerabilities of capital that these reveal. It takes a global tour of the massive infrastructure corridors that are being planned to enable further economies of scale in the extraction, transportation and production of resources and consumer goods by compressing space by time. It argues that dominant forms of industrial capital cannot easily expand without massive expenditure on these corridors. But the planners' plans are bumping up against the frontiers of traditional infrastructure finance. The money simply is not available without tapping a wider pool of finance beyond the state, private banks and multilateral institutions: global capital markets are the target source, Public–Private Partnerships the inducement, and infrastructure-as-asset-class the currently favoured (if often faltering) means of delivery.

Chapter 6 reflects on the challenges that the reconfiguration of infrastructure poses for activism. The push for greater private sector involvement in financing and operating infrastructure has sparked resistance from many quarters, including trade unions, environmental and human rights campaigners, and other social movements. But in many instances, such responses are weakened by the hollowing out of many of the traditional cross-cutting, community-embedded vehicles for mobilising for social change. Instead, advocacy is increasingly channelled through consultancies or single-issue, non-governmental organisations, many of which have become quasi-corporate franchises whose relationship to their political base is primarily driven by fund-raising. As a result, it is difficult to move beyond 'reformist reforms' (which tend to undermine long-term movement-building) so as to push instead for 'non-reformist reforms' (which open up strategic space for genuine change). Challenging the trajectory of contemporary infrastructure finance – and the inequalities and injustices it gives rise to – is likely to be more fruitful where it is part of a wider effort to build or strengthen commons-focused resistance to accumulation.

Note

1 In 2014 the biggest gap in the US was at media company Discovery Communications, where CEO David Zaslav earned $156.1 million, nearly 1,951 times the firm's median salary of $80,000 (Che 2015).

Chapter 2

A study in financial extraction: Lesotho's national referral hospital

Let us start with a concrete example of infrastructure as financial extraction to illustrate the types of deals being set up, quite lawfully, that serve to siphon money towards the wealthy. This is no easy task. Commercial confidentiality ensures that many of the financial arrangements underlying the deals remain secret, but detailed figures for many deals have emerged. One example is a controversial Public–Private Partnership for three filter clinics and a new 425-bed hospital in Maseru, the capital of Lesotho, one of the poorest countries in the world (Lister 2011). The new hospital, the Queen 'Mamohato Memorial Hospital, was the first in Africa to be built under a PPP contract and the first of its kind for a low-income country anywhere in the world. The World Bank's International Finance Corporation, which advised on the deal, sees the project as a model to be replicated across the continent. But the international development group Oxfam has criticised the PPP for its alleged adverse impacts on Lesotho's healthcare budget (Marriott 2014). As a result of the ensuing controversy, considerable detail has emerged on the deal to supplement what had already come into the public domain (PWC 2013).

2.1 The consortium

The new hospital, which replaced the publicly owned and operated Queen Elizabeth II hospital, is run by a private consortium, Tsepong, which was also responsible under the PPP for designing, building and financing the whole project.[1] Tsepong is currently headed by the South African private medical multinational Netcare, which owns 40 per cent of the consortium (Firman and Litlhakanyane 2010). Netcare also runs hospitals in the UK and South Africa. A subsidiary, Netcare KwaZulu, was fined $700,000 in 2010 in South Africa for illegally selling human kidneys, a number of them purchased from children (Netcare 2010).

The other shareholders in Tsepong (known as the 'Lesotho Economic Empowerment' (LEE) shareholders) are:

- *Excel Health* (20 per cent), a private company, registered in Lesotho, that, according to recent court documents, was 'established in 2005 by a group of medical doctors to serve as a vehicle for furthering their common business interests' (Lesotho Court of Appeal 2013);
- *Afri'nnai* (20 per cent), 'an investment company for doctors and medical specialists from South Africa' (PWC 2013);
- *Women Investment Company* (10 per cent), an investment company for Basotho women; and
- *D10 Investments* (10 per cent), the investment division of the local Chamber of Commerce.

In August 2015 three of Netcare's partners in the consortium were reported to be seeking a court order to place the hospital under judicial management for six months and for an official investigation into Netcare for corruption (Kabi 2015b), an allegation that Netcare vigorously denies (Kabi 2015a). The directors of Tsepong have refused to sign the consortium's annual financial statements since 2012, arguing that a number of payments need to be explained. The failure to approve the consortium's financial statements has been held to place Tsepong in breach of the Public–Private Partnership agreement with the Government of Lesotho (High Court of South Africa 2015).

2.2   The Public–Private Partnership deal

Under the 18-year PPP contract between the Government of Lesotho and Tsepong, the consortium is required to provide clinical services at the new hospital and three filter clinics, 'including staffing, medicine, general expenses, preventive maintenance, ambulances, and management services' (Boston University 2013). Netcare is responsible for the operation and management of the project; Excel Health and Afri'nnai for supplying doctors; the Women Investment Company for supplying housekeeping and 'soft' services; and D10 for transportation and other services.

To cover the consortium's contracted expenses, the Government of Lesotho pays Tsepong an index-linked annual 'unitary payment', which, in 2015, amounted to nearly $30 million.[2] The exact breakdown of this payment into capital outlay and operating expenses is considered proprietary and confidential information. However, it has reportedly been calculated (in part) on the estimated cost of treating up to 20,000 in-patients and 310,000 out-patients a year. If more patients are treated, additional payments kick in. In 2014 the extra services provided by Tsepong amounted to just under $6 million (Netcare 2015; Khaketla 2015).

2.3 Budgetary impacts

Even before the new hospital opened its doors, the World Bank hailed it a 'success' that would result in 'vastly improved facilities, medical services, and patient care' (Faustino Coelho and O'Farrell 2009), while being affordable for the government. But a detailed report by two non-governmental organisations, Oxfam International and the Consumers' Protection Association (Lesotho) (CPAL), paints a very different picture (Marriott 2014). According to this 2014 report, the PPP hospital and its three filter clinics cost three times more to run than the old public hospital: as a result, the PPP is allegedly eating up 51 per cent of the total government health budget, a figure that the groups predict will rise considerably by 2017. The report warns that primary and secondary healthcare in rural areas, 'where mortality rates are rising and where three-quarters of the population live', are increasingly starved of funding, making the bias in favour of tertiary care (already long identified as a problem in public health) even worse.

Netcare rejects the findings of this report, denying that the project will consume half of Lesotho's health budget (the company puts the figure at 35 per cent, thus slightly more expensive than the old hospital). It also describes the PPP as 'a major success story in terms of significantly widening access to quality healthcare for the people of Lesotho and providing patients with healthcare services previously not available' (Netcare 2014a).

In May 2015 Lesotho's Minister of Finance confirmed that the government was considering building a new public hospital in Maseru to reduce the number of patients being referred to the PPP hospital in order 'to ease the burden' on the government's health budget (Khaketla 2015).

2.4 Who takes the risks?

The World Bank claims that the PPP was structured to ensure 'maximum risk transfer to the private operator' (Faustino Coelho and O'Farrell 2009). Superficially, this might appear to be the case. The total capital expenditure for the project has been put at $153.1 million

(PWC 2013). According to Netcare, 33 per cent of the finance came from public funds and 67 per cent from private funds (Netcare 2014a). Others give a slightly lower percentage for the private sector financing – 62 per cent (Boston University 2013) – either way, the private sector would appear to be taking the major share of the financial risk.

But, as in many PPPs, appearances are often highly deceptive (see Box 2.1 'When public is private and private is public'). In this case,

---

Box 2.1 When public is private and private is public

One justification often given for Public–Private Partnerships (PPPs) is that they bring private money into the financing of infrastructure, thereby relieving the public purse. But in many cases, what appears to be 'private' is in fact 'public' or quasi-public. For example, India's Infrastructure Leasing & Financial Services Limited (IL&FS), which lends money for infrastructure development, including a number of PPPs, is a private company. Yet its largest shareholder is the state-owned Life Insurance Corporation Ltd, while other state entities, such as the Central Bank of India and the State Bank of India, are also shareholders. Similarly, Britain's official development finance institution, CDC Group, which has widely invested in infrastructure, is wholly owned by the UK's Department for International Development (DfID) but run as a private company, with DfID held at 'arm's length'.

This trend is part of a wider move by many states to remodel their public sectors (where they have not been privatised) on 'business lines', transforming public bodies into profit-seeking centres run according to commercial practices. As a consequence, the distinction between public and private finance is often blurred to the point where the two categories cease to have much meaning. The Lesotho case (see main text) is an example. Indeed, close examination of the financing of many PPPs reveals that the bulk of the money often comes not from the private sector operator but from the public sector, albeit often channelled through publicly owned 'private' companies. One analysis of water project PPPs in India, for example, found that the private sector operator had 'not brought in any significant equity contribution' and that the projects were funded 'through other means'. A World Bank review of five Indian PPP water projects in 2014 similarly notes that 'All the projects reviewed rely substantially on public funds.' In the case of the city of Mysore's six-year distribution contract with private operator JUSCO to rehabilitate and improve the city's water supply, no capital at all came in from the private partner.

Sources: Leys 2001; CSE India 2011; World Bank 2014b

closer scrutiny reveals that the vast majority of the finance is either guaranteed or put up by the public. The amount actually put in by the consortium is just under $7.6 million (Netcare 2015) – some 5 per cent of the total capital expenditure. So who did put up the money? And who took the risks?

On the public side, the Lesotho government made 'significant up-front payments' (PWC 2013) for the project in the form of a direct capital payment of $47.5 million towards the construction costs and an additional payment of $10.2 million for 'enabling works', such as bringing a sewage system and electricity to the hospital site. The World Bank also provided a grant of $6 million. So, in total, the public made payments of $63.7 million, for which it took all the risks.

On the 'private' side, the consortium says it put up just $689,000 in equity (the multinational accounting and auditing firm PWC put the figure at $474,665, based in part on information from the consortium, but let's not quibble about a few thousand dollars) (Netcare 2015; PWC 2013). In addition, Tsepong's shareholders have made loans of $6.9 million (Netcare 2015). The consortium also received a loan of some $100 million from the Development Bank of Southern Africa (DBSA) (Netcare 2010). (Again, there are discrepancies over the figures: others put the loan at $95 million (PWC 2013), but let's proceed on the basis of Netcare's slightly higher figures.) On the face of it, then, the consortium took the financial risk for approximately $107.6 million of the total $153 million capital investment.

But dig a little deeper and a different picture emerges. It turns out that the DBSA loan agreement was guaranteed by the Government of Lesotho, which would be responsible for the loan in the event of a default on payment.[3] The loan money went to the consortium and is counted (officially) as part of its investment in the project; but, in reality, it is the Government of Lesotho's debt, albeit an off-balance-sheet one. Arguably, in terms of risk, it should therefore be placed on the 'public' side of the equation, all the more so given that the repayments are guaranteed by the government through its contract with Tsepong.

To confuse the (not so) neat public/private divide still further, DBSA is a public bank, not a private one. So the money that was put at risk was doubly public: first, because it was money from a public institution; and second, because it was guaranteed by the Government of Lesotho.

So, if common sense rather than company law and accounting practices is the measure, 95 per cent of the money for the project could be said to be 'public' money (see Exhibit 2.1). Certainly

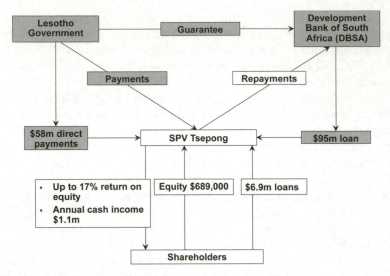

Exhibit 2.1 Who takes the risks?
The PPP for the Queen 'Mamohato Memorial Hospital in Lesotho is said to ensure 'maximum risk transfer to the private operator'. Is this the case? The diagram above sets out the financial structure for the project. The grey boxes detail monies that either come directly or indirectly from public funds, or which are guaranteed by the Government of Lesotho. The white boxes are monies where the risk falls entirely on the private sector consortium. Thus 95 per cent of the risk would appear to fall on the public, not the private, sector.

95 per cent of the risk would appear to fall on the public, not 33 per cent as official figures suggest. This is particularly worrying given that Tsepong is reported to have defaulted on a number of its loan repayments because the Ministry of Health has been struggling to pay its monthly unitary fees (Marriott 2014).

2.5 Rates of return

According to Oxfam and CPAL, the PPP behind the Queen 'Mamohato Memorial Hospital was structured to generate '25 per cent of return on equity for the PPP shareholders and a total pro-jected cash income 7.6 times higher than their original investment' (Marriott 2014). Netcare (2014a) rejects these figures, maintaining that the 'investment was made with an expectation of earning a return that compares with the norm on similar hospital PFI projects in the UK of between 13 per cent and 18 per cent'[4] (just to be clear: the cited UK percentages are annual returns).

The consortium has confirmed that 'the real return was forecasted at no more than 17 per cent' (Netcare 2015)[5] – thus towards the higher end of the spectrum for similar (highly profitable) projects in the UK. But even at 17 per cent, rather than the 25 per cent cited by Oxfam and CPAL, the annual returns on an investment where the risk is, in the final analysis, borne almost entirely by the public are of questionable justification. At 17 per cent, the value of the consortium's $107.6 million (largely government-guaranteed) investment would rise by $18.3 million a year. Over the lifetime of the PPP, the projected return would be almost $330 million. As for cash income, the consortium projects returns of just under $1.1 million a year, which amount to $19.8 million over the PPP's lifetime (Netcare 2015). All in all, not bad for an upfront investment of at most $7.6 million dollars.

2.6 Who gets the profits?

As of 2014 no profits had been distributed to the consortium's shareholders (Netcare 2014a).[6] But, assuming that the PPP makes the consortium its intended profits, will they remain in Lesotho to be invested on behalf of *all* of Lesotho's two million people, not just those who are invested in Tsepong, as they might be if the hospital was run as a publicly owned entity? And, if not, who will reap the financial rewards?

At least 60 per cent of profits and increased share value will go to Netcare's Lesotho-based partner investors (even though Afri'nnai is based in South Africa, the majority of its shareholders have Lesotho citizenship).[7] But Netcare's shareholders will also benefit. The majority of these investors (as of mid-2015) are institutions; namely, banks (5.35 per cent), insurance companies (7.73 per cent), pension funds and medical aid societies (37.95 per cent) and collective investment vehicles or mutual funds (40.11 per cent) (Netcare 2014b). As detailed in Exhibit 2.2, the top ten investors, as of August 2015, were all South African-based.

It isn't the poor in Lesotho, those at the bottom of the national and global wealth pyramid, who own Netcare's institutional investors, nor are they likely to. It is, by and large, the 1% in South Africa. So much of the financial extraction enabled by the PPP is not simply from Lesotho's public purse: it is also geographical – *out* of Lesotho and *up* to the 1% in South Africa and beyond.

Undoubtedly, the new hospital is better equipped and, judged by international standards, of a higher quality than the hospital it replaced. But it may be assumed that this would equally have been the case if the government had funded the new hospital directly

Exhibit 2.2 Netcare's ten top shareholders in 2015

Institutional shareholder	Percentage of shares held	Location of headquarters
Public Investment Corporation Ltd	16.2%	South Africa. Government-owned private limited company.
Allan Gray Unit Trust Management (RF) (PTY) Ltd	3.69%	South Africa. Allan Gray is the 'largest privately owned and independent asset manager in Southern Africa'.
Netcare Fund	3.62%	South Africa.
Liberty Group Ltd (Investment Portfolio)	3.14%	South Africa. Privately owned pan-African financial services company.
The Vanguard Group, Inc.	2.95%	USA. One of the world's largest investment management companies.
Investment Solutions Ltd	2.52%	South Africa. Investment management company.
Stanlib Asset Management Ltd	2.08%	South Africa. Asset manager.
Old Mutual Life Assurance Co. South Africa Ltd	1.69%	South Africa. Life assurance and retirement fund company.
Norges Bank Investment Management	1.53%	Norway. Manages the Norwegian government's sovereign wealth funds – the Government Pension Fund Global – on behalf of the Norwegian Ministry of Finance.
Sanlam Investment Management (Pty) Ltd	1.34%	South Africa. Financial services group.

Sources: 4-Traders 2015 and company websites

rather than through the PPP.[8] The big difference is that the public money used to finance the project would have remained just that: public money. All profits (not just the taxes paid by the consortium) would have been returned to the Lesotho exchequer to be used for all the people of Lesotho. By transforming a portion of that public money into private profit, the PPP does more than just enrich the consortium's shareholders: it also strips the extracted public monies of their public purpose, unshackling them from previous restrictions on how and where they can be spent and for whose benefit. Once privatised, the profits, although originating from public funds, are free to roam far and wide in search of further profit, even in activities that may directly harm the people of Lesotho.[9]

Netcare and Tsepong do not deny that the Lesotho hospital PPP generates profit for the consortium; but they strongly reject the suggestion that the PPP serves to extract wealth for the already wealthy –

Box 2.2 Financial extraction? Netcare and Tsepong response

In a 'Right of Reply' response to a draft of this chapter, Netcare and Tsepong took issue with the view that arrangements to finance infrastructure 'are being set up, quite lawfully, to siphon money towards the already wealthy'.

Referring to the Lesotho hospital PPP, the companies responded as follows:

'We consider [this statement] as a material blunder for the following key reasons:

• The procurement process was predicated on the healthcare needs of the community, implying that the procurement process was based on a needs analysis with clearly defined requirements. The project is therefore the product of a decade's worth of research with the only purpose being the improvement of healthcare service delivery to the Basotho community;

• The procurement process followed a competitive tendering process where the outcome of the competition was an unknown, only to be determined by the best value for money proposal. Any qualified bidder could be awarded the PPP agreement and this would only have been executed if it met the project requirements and offered a value for money solution;

• The service fees paid by the Government of Lesotho ('GoL') returns 'a monument for the nation' at the expiry of the PPP agreement. The operator may only occupy the facility for a fixed period pursuant to the concession agreement and never takes ownership of the assets. Hence, the acceptable project specific finance arrangements; and

• To describe the project as a mechanism whereby money is being siphoned 'towards the already wealthy' will be regarded as an insult, especially to the majority or 60% shareholders of the consortium and paradoxically the opposite applies, both in respect of reasons for participation and financial reward'.

Source: Netcare 2015

a view they describe as 'an insult' to the majority of its shareholders (see Box 2.2 'Financial extraction? Netcare and Tsepong response') (Netcare 2015). They insist that the 'only purpose' of the PPP is 'the improvement of healthcare service delivery to the Basotho community' (Netcare 2015). This confuses the issue: financial extraction is not about the social purpose intentions of a project, but about the flows of wealth through it and who gets to enjoy them. And the figures – which Netcare and Tsepong have confirmed – speak for themselves. The consortium stands to make millions out of the project – and a sizeable chunk of this will be for the 1%.

There is nothing unlawful in such financial extraction. On the contrary, the companies and investment funds involved have a legal duty to maximise returns to their shareholders. And that, of course, is precisely the problem. For, as we shall see in the next chapter, the profit-seeking lens through which finance views 'infrastructure' transforms it into something that is unrecognisable to the rest of us – at our expense.

Notes

1 Tsepong and Netcare, Tsepong's majority shareholder, were invited to comment on a draft of this chapter. In response they clarified a number of facts, for which I am grateful. They also made plain their fundamental disagreement with the chapter's approach. They stressed that their comments 'should … not be construed as a direct or indirect approval, by any party, for any information related to the project [the chapter] to be published' (Netcare 2015).

2 Netcare and Tsepong (2015) give the figure of $29,460,501.

3 Netcare and Tsepong accept that the Government of Lesotho (GoL) 'provided surety to the DBSA'. However, they contend that 'in the event of a default on payment, GoL may have the obligation to meet commitments to the DBSA but in return it will retain ownership of the hospital, filter clinics and related assets. The "surety" provided to the DBSA compared with the value of the asset to be recovered offers excellent loan to value returns, hence a very acceptable risk: reward exposure' (Netcare 2015). But it is standard commercial practice that, in the event of a default, the secured lender will take control of the asset. Such control of the asset is not a concession by a kind borrower but a two-way relation of advantage: the lender gains security and the borrower gains from being charged much lower rates of interest than would be the case if the loan was unsecured.

4 Netcare and Tsepong now state in addition: 'The project return of 25 per cent is misleading at best, based on nominal values over the long-term project period' (Netcare 2015).

5 Netcare and Tsepong point out that the return is weighted 'in favour of the Lesotho Economic Empowerment shareholders, measured over the lifetime of the agreement'. Consequently, 'Netcare's weighted return, albeit a 40 per cent consortium member, is lower than its 40 per cent entitlement' (Netcare 2015).

6 Netcare has stated that the majority of profits from its own holdings in associate companies, such as Tsepong, are 'ordinarily retained and reinvested to further its healthcare operations and to grow market share' (Netcare 2015).

7 Netcare and Tsepong state: 'Up to 60 per cent of shareholding is effectively Lesotho based and will increase over the lifetime of the agreement. The return mechanism leverages returns in favour of LEE shareholders denuding Netcare's effective 40 per cent settlement … It cannot be excluded that "the poor" may acquire 100% of the issued shares of Tsepong' (Netcare 2015).

8 Netcare and Tsepong suggest that this might not be the case. They argue that the current standards of delivery are a result of its ability to 'provide significant cross pollination benefits through procurement, mentorship and training' (Netcare 2015).

9 Netcare and Tsepong comment: 'The public remains the owner of the facilities and the agreement provides flexibility to either terminate the agreement or improve the value for money proposal if any recalibration is required or if any party is unsatisfied with the project deliverables' (Netcare 2015). This misses the point: the profits from the project are not public, even though they may have been derived from putting public money to work. In addition, it would appear that terminating the contract is a less viable response for the Lesotho government to the financial burden on its health budget created by the PPP than building a new public hospital (Khaketla 2015).

Chapter 3

Infrastructure as financial extraction

> He goes on Sunday to the church to hear the Parson shout.
> He puts a penny in the plate and takes a pound note out
> And drops a conscience-stricken tear in case he is found out.
> (Parody of Oliver Goldsmith's *The Village Blacksmith*, Anonymous)

3.1 Infrastructure through finance's eyes

Ask an ordinary person in the street in any large city in the industrialised world to react to the word 'infrastructure' and the reply (in so far as ordinary people even think about 'infrastructure') is likely to include 'roads', 'railways', 'airports', 'bridges', 'water pipes', 'sewers', 'drains', 'lighting', 'heating', 'power stations', 'pylons' and 'internet cables'. Some might add in 'libraries', 'parks', 'sports grounds', 'hospitals', 'clinics' and 'schools'. Extending the analysis beyond bricks and mortar, phrases such as 'used by all', 'servicing the community', 'enhancing public life' or 'what keeps a community functioning' may emerge. Some may agree with New York public official Herbert Muschamp (1994) that 'infrastructure' is 'shorthand for the structural underpinnings of the public realm' or with academics Vicki Elmer and Adam Leigland (2014, p. 6) that infrastructure is the built foundations of our cities and towns that 'we cannot finance or build on our own' and that 'we must join together as a society to plan, finance and care for'. Others may like the description of infrastructure as the physical 'sinews' of society (Tarr 2005, p. 97). But three phrases are unlikely to crop up: 'assets', 'income streams' and 'returns'.

Not so when investors are asked the same question. Surf the internet sites where finance talks to finance, or read the briefings prepared by City fund managers or Wall Street's shadow bankers, and a very different approach to 'infrastructure' emerges. The vocabulary appears the same ('roads', 'power stations', 'clinics', and so on); and there are the same warm phrases about the public role of infrastructure (the global accountancy firm KPMG begins a report on infrastructure with the statement: 'Infrastructure is part of the social conscience' (KPMG 2014)): but the words no longer have their vernacular meaning and belong to a different language. A 'road' does not mean a 'road', but a 'toll road' – an altogether different entity. A hospital is not where the sick go to be healed, but a conveyer belt of patients whose processing rings a cash till. And, as with all private investments, the '*in*' in 'infrastructure *in*vestment' is not about putting money *in*to society through improving the facilities and services that people rely on, or providing them where they do not yet exist: it is about taking money *out* of such facilities and services.

Yield, not physical characteristics, becomes the determinant of what is or is not an infrastructure asset. Jean Perarnaud, managing director of the Private Infrastructure team at Partners Group, a tax haven-based Swiss investment management firm, captures the approach in an interview with *Infrastructure Investor*: 'For us, infrastructure is stable, contracted cash flow for the long term' (Kranc 2014, p. 5). Not schools, note; nor clinics, roads, power plants, sewage treatment plants, nor networks of piped water: but contracted cash flow. Finance does not quibble as to whether the contract is between two private sector companies (an oil producer and an oil distributor, for example) or between a private company and a public entity. But on one point it is clear: without the guarantee of a contract, infrastructure (in finance's sense of the term) is not infrastructure. Perarnaud is adamant: 'You could have a pipeline that you don't want to touch because there are no contractual rights on it and it is completely market-exposed to price. *These are the sort of things we don't consider infrastructure*' (Kranc 2014, p. 5, emphasis added).

Here one surely needs to take a deep breath and a swig of Alice in Wonderland's 'Drink Me' potion. For it is only when mundane preoccupations with bricks and mortar have been shrunk to next to nothing that one can enter the space that finance calls infrastructure. Once through the door, a vast array of unfamiliar platforms are revealed, some already constructed, others being cobbled together using the building blocks of guaranteed internal rates of return, Take or Pay contracts, tax breaks, credit enhancements, securitisations, carbon credits, arbitration clauses, and other legal and financial mysteries (of which more later). It takes a while to adjust one's eyes to the scene and to absorb what is different about its apparent familiarities. For this is a domain in which what is recognisably 'infrastructure' for the rest of us (an oil pipeline, to use Perarnaud's example) is not necessarily 'infrastructure' for the Humpty Dumpties of finance; and in which what is clearly not 'infrastructure' in the vernacular sense (a wetland or a forest) can become 'infrastructure' with the stroke of a pen on a contract. The differences go beyond mere differences of definition. Finance's infrastructure-as-yield embodies a political, economic and social trajectory that is entirely different to that of 'infrastructure-as-society's-sinews', with profound implications for what facilities and services get financed, how they are financed, who enjoys access to them and who does not. It also ushers in new forms of violence (the ghosts of capitalism again) as humans and non-humans are transformed into 'stable, contracted cash flow' (see Box 3.1 'The violence of "contracted income streams"'). Only when this is grasped does the Cheshire Cat that is infrastructure-as-finance-intends-it make itself visible. And the grin that remains after the Cheshire Cat has vanished is the several hundreds of billions of dollars extracted every year for the benefit of the 1%.

So what are the platforms that are being constructed? How do they work to extract wealth? And how much wealth is being extracted?

Box 3.1 The violence of 'contracted income streams'

'Contracted income streams' sound so innocuous. Who could blame finance for seeking them? But their construction can entail considerable violence.

To make the profits they seek, private sector operators of public infrastructure routinely raise tariffs, leaving many poorer people without access to water or electricity. One IMF study found that 62 per cent of all renegotiated Public–Private Partnership (PPP) contracts resulted in higher tariffs. In Uganda, for example, Umeme, a privatised Ugandan power distributor, secured a price rise of 24 per cent in 2005 and then sought a further 37 per cent rise in 2007, leading to a court challenge by the Uganda Electricity Users Association (UEUA). Many poorer Ugandans were forced to steal electricity from the grid because of the high prices; the reported response of one Umeme manager was to call for their execution.

To speed up the throughput of patients in privately run hospitals, sick people have been subjected to management techniques borrowed from industry. In the case of Hinchingbrooke, the UK's only wholly privately run NHS hospital, a waiting time management system first pioneered by retail giant Argos was introduced in the Accident and Emergency department.

Patient care was judged so inadequate that the hospital was eventually placed in 'special measures' by the UK's Care Quality Commission.

As finance moves to profit from areas of social care that have previously been largely the province of families and communities, the ways in which people view each other and themselves must also be transformed. Work by academics such as Paula Hyde of Durham University has documented how, in order to transform older people into long-term income streams, society's attitude to old age must be hardened and the elderly must begin to define themselves not by their lived lives but by their failing health. If they are to fit into the routine of care homes, they must be deracinated from their previous lives and their sense of independence constantly undermined through institutionalised practices.

Contracted income streams can also do much violence to democracy where they are negotiated in private and result in projects that lock society into a trajectory that cannot be reversed without paying companies massive compensation.

Sources: Hall 2007; Hyde *et al.* 2007; Owen 2015; Zacune, 2006

3.2 Guarantee me: piracy of the public by the private

For many people, the notion of infrastructure as 'contracted income streams' is both alien and intellectually intimidating. It is so at odds with a common sense view of infrastructure that there is an understandable tendency to brush it to one side and engage on more familiar ground. What are the specific outcomes of individual projects and investments? What are the environmental or human rights impacts? How are labour rights affected? Were affected communities consulted? Have they been compensated for loss of land? Was the project tainted by corruption? Who is investing and how might they be lobbied to stop or improve the project? Are the contracts open to public scrutiny? Who will benefit from the project? Who will lose out?

Such questions – and the political organising that accompanies them – are central to ensuring that concerns over social and environmental justice are not swept aside in the push to build new infrastructure or privatise existing facilities. But there is a danger that a narrow focus on the familiar leaves unchallenged the broader project that finance is constructing through 'infrastructure' – enabling, rather than deflecting, its injustice-generating trajectory. With an estimated $4 trillion or more of 'private' money now invested in finance's 'infrastructure' (see Box 3.2 'Infrastructure: how much is

> **Box 3.2 Infrastructure: how much is invested?**
>
> The volume of money swirling around the 'infrastructure investment space' globally probably amounts to several trillions of dollars. One snapshot measure is the amount of money invested by institutional investors, such as pension funds, insurance companies, sovereign wealth funds and philanthropic foundations. In 2010 such investors had an estimated $600–700 billion (or 1 per cent of their total assets under management) invested in dedicated infrastructure funds. But if the stocks and bonds held by institutional investors *outside* of such funds were also taken into account, the total investment would have been an estimated $1.4 trillion.
>
> Add in the investments of 'retail investors' (that is, individuals who make investments on their own account) and the total sum invested just in 'economic infrastructure' is likely to be in the low trillions of dollars. Research by RREEF Securities has put the stock market value of the world's major listed 'infrastructure' companies at $3 trillion, of which $875 billion consists of 'pure-play' infrastructure companies (energy distribution, toll roads, airports and the like) and the rest of companies associated with infrastructure (engineering and construction, power generation, shipping).
>
> But even this $3 trillion figure is likely to be a low estimate. If the net is widened to include companies that make more than 50 per cent of their income from 'economic infrastructure' – the majority of them in developing countries – the numbers are higher still. And if companies in social and commodity infrastructure are taken into account, the amounts of money going into the infrastructure asset class swell still further.
>
> But by how much is pure guesswork. No aggregate figures are publicly available.
>
> Sources: Della Croce and Yermo 2013; Inderst 2013; Rothballer and Kaserer 2012; RREEF 2011

invested?') – and more predicted to follow as infrastructure moves to the top of many investors' shopping lists – it would seem important to explore what 'contracted income streams' entail in practice and how they are now central to the emergence of infrastructure as a supercharged vehicle for accumulation.

The past history of private investment in infrastructure provides a useful starting point. Go back a century and a half and 'contracted income' was, as today, the central demand (make no mistake: it is a demand) of investors. India's early railways may have been built with private money, amply subsidised by land grants and the like, but the investors enriched themselves largely through contracts that amounted to licensed larceny. Most infamously, the colonial government guaranteed railway companies a 5 per cent annual profit, underwritten by Indian, not British, taxpayers. The result was a massive transfer of wealth from Indians to investors abroad, the majority in Britain, many of them ex-colonial officials. The British government knew it was a scam – and a costly one: it eventually spent about £50 million on paying out the calls on the guarantees it had made, compared with a total British investment of some £150 million – but it could do little to avoid paying up: the contracts locked in the guarantees for a 99-year period. William Thomas Thornton, Secretary of Public Works at the India Office, railed that the scheme was nothing more than 'private enterprise at public risk' (Jack 2014), while Sir John Lawrence, the British Governor-General of India from 1864 to 1869, lamented:

> The Government of India has for several years been striving to induce capitalists to undertake construction of railways in India at their own risk, and on their responsibility with a minimum of Government interference. But the attempt has entirely failed, and it has become obvious that no capital can be obtained for such undertakings otherwise than under a guarantee of interest, fully equal to that which the Government would have to pay if it borrowed on its own account.
>
> (Bogart and Chaudhary 2012, p. 7)

Such looting was by no means confined to India. Similar guarantees – some even more generous than in India – were also the norm for extractive railway investments in Argentina, Brazil, Peru, Uruguay, Venezuela, South Africa, Sri Lanka, Canada, France, Germany, Russia and the Ottoman Empire. In Argentina, which had been experiencing an economic boom, the guarantees proved so onerous that they 'brought the whole fragile edifice of the Argentine economic miracle to ruin' (Lewis 1983, p. 86).

Box 3.3 The economic metabolism of loans and guarantees – a word or two from Rosa Luxemburg

It is now just over a century since Rosa Luxemburg, the revolutionary German socialist and Marxist thinker, published *The Accumulation of Capital*. Written in just four months (a period Luxemburg, who was later murdered by right-wing thugs, described as belonging to 'the happiest of my life'), the book sought to understand the dynamics behind the imperial conquests of Britain, France, Germany and other colonial powers.

Her thesis was that capitalism is inherently driven to expand into areas where there are non-capitalist social formations and to absorb them. This, she argued, was necessary because there was never sufficient demand to purchase all the goods produced at any one time by capitalists: and without such demand, the surplus value needed to keep the accumulation process going could not be fully realised. Additional demand, she concluded, must therefore be generated by incorporating those living outside the circuits of capital accumulation. This was accomplished in part through military conquest but also through making loans to create 'new opportunities to beget and realise surplus value'.

One example that Luxemburg explored in some depth was the loans made by Germany to Turkey to build a railway line from Konya in Turkey to Baghdad. To repay the loans, the Turkish government assigned the tithes collected from peasants in a number of districts as security. These tithes were generally 'paid' in the form of wheat, which was then sold by a local tithe collector, who handed the money (less a commission) to the government.

'This money', writes Luxemburg, 'is nothing but converted peasant grain; it was not even produced as a commodity. But now, as a state guarantee, it serves towards paying for the construction and operation of railways.' In this process, 'further means of production of German origin are used, and so the peasant grain of Asia, converted into money, also serves to turn into cash the surplus value that has been extorted from the German workers.' The money 'rolls from the hands of the Turkish government into the coffers of the Deutsche Bank, and here it accumulates, as capitalist surplus value, in the form of promoters' profits, royalties, dividends and interests in the accounts of Messrs. Gwinner, Siemens, Stinnes and their fellow directors, of the shareholders and clients of the Deutsche Bank and the whole intricate system of its subsidiary companies'.

At bottom, argues Luxemburg, it is 'an exchange between German capital and Asiatic peasant economy, an exchange performed under state compulsion'.

The same may, perhaps, be said for some PPPs, for the user fees collected through PPP contracts (and the guarantees that stand behind them) are similarly collected, in part, from many whose production still falls outside of capitalist labour relations.

Sources: Luxemburg 2003; Schmidt 2011, 2014

3.3 Public–Private Partnerships: bring on the (private) profits

Today, the colonels who funded their retirement off the backs of Indian taxpayers would salivate over the array of guaranteed income streams that finance is developing through infrastructure. One field of experimentation that has proved particularly fruitful (for the private sector, if not for the public) is that of Public–Private Partnerships or PPPs, a back door route to privatisation that emerged in the 1990s as an alternative to outright divestiture of state-owned and -operated infrastructure assets. Proponents cite a long (and generally faux) history. The unthreatening, even bucolic, origins of a fifteenth-century concession granted to a nobleman to charge fees for goods transported on the Rhine are evoked ad nauseam; less is made of the Elizabethan pirates who were licensed by the English throne as 'privateers' to loot Spanish galleons carrying gold from South America.

In their modern incarnation, which has evolved considerably in function and form from its various historical antecedents, PPPs arose partly as 'an accounting trick, a way round the government's own constraints on public borrowing' (Hall 2015) and partly as response to the lukewarm financial returns that followed the privatisation of much publicly owned infrastructure in the 1980s and 1990s.[1] Opportunistic fortunes were certainly made from outright divestitures, particularly in the oil and gas sector, as whole sectors of the economy were sold off, often at fire sale prices to those without obvious means but with powerful political connections. But those who sought to make a financial killing by running newly sold public service infrastructure often came a cropper. They simply could not make the profits they sought through relying on user fees from the pesky poor.

Many investors quickly found themselves nursing loss-making investments and facing increasing public hostility over rising user fees and declining services. One study of privatised utilities in 31 developing countries found that 80 per cent 'experienced negative changes in profitability' (Cook and Uchida 2004, p. 9).[2] As a result, by 2002 all the major multinational companies with water supply contracts in developing countries were looking for an exit. As UK water company Biwater explained after withdrawing from a major water project in Zimbabwe, 'Investors need to be convinced that they will get reasonable returns ... From a social point of view, these kinds of projects are viable but unfortunately from a private sector point of view they are not' (Hall and Lobina 2008). Indeed, by 2005 even the World Bank was describing infrastructure privatisation as 'oversold and misunderstood' (Kessides 2004, p. 6), although this did not stop the bank from continuing to impose privatisation pro-grammes as part of its loan conditions.

PPPs have provided the way forward for the privatisers. Contracts (in the form of PPP-based leases, concessions and management agreements) rather than outright divestments are now a prime means through which the private sector gains access to public service income streams. The PPP contracts take various forms: some involve the construction and operation of new infrastructure, others the provision of services from existing facilities; in some, the ownership of the underlying asset is ultimately transferred to the private sector operator, in others it remains with the state. Acronyms abound – from BOOs to BOTs, BLOTS, BOOTs, BROTS and LDOs (see Exhibit 3.1). With a BOT (build–operate–transfer), for example, a private sector entity finances construction and is repaid by the state, in regular instalments, for the use of the buildings and services provided under a facilities management contract. The facility passes to the government when the operating contract ends, or at some other pre-specified time. With a BOO (build–operate–own), ownership remains with the private entity but the contract provides for various forms of government support

Exhibit 3.1 Major types of Public–Private Partnerships (PPPs)

Schemes	How they work
Build–own–operate (BOO) Build–develop–operate (BDO)	The private sector partner is contracted to design, build, develop, operate and manage an asset. Ownership remains with the private partner.
Buy–build–operate (BBO) Lease–develop–operate (LDO)	The private sector partner buys or leases an existing asset from the government and undertakes to renovate, modernise or expand it. The private partner operates the asset under a contract with the government.
Build–operate–transfer (BOT) Build–own–operate–transfer (BOOT) Build–rent–own–transfer (BROT) Build–lease–operate–transfer (BLOT) Build–transfer–operate (BTO)	The private sector partner designs and builds an asset, operates it, and then transfers it to the government at a pre-specified time, usually the end of the contract. The private partner may subsequently rent or lease the asset from the government.

Source: adapted from IMF 2006

during the contract period. With an LDO (lease–develop–operate), an existing asset is leased from the government, with the private entity contracted to renovate and operate it.

Multilateral development banks, governments and neoliberal-inclined think tanks are currently pushing PPPs as the vanguard vehicle for attracting private investment into infrastructure (see Box 3.4 'PPPs: pushing private profits'). The latest justification (which, as we shall see in Chapter 5, should be treated with considerable scepticism) is that private finance is needed to bridge the perceived gulf between available public money and the 'dozens of trillions' (Inderst 2009, p. 5) that need to be spent on infrastructure over the next twenty years. Much is also claimed (spuriously) for the efficiencies that PPPs will supposedly bring to infrastructure management. Less is said about the efficiency of the private sector

---

Box 3.4 PPPs: pushing private profits

For the World Bank and other multilateral development banks, Public–Private Partnerships (PPPs) are the vehicles of choice for financing and providing public services. Now used in more than 134 developing countries, PPPs are resurgent after a slowdown in the aftermath of the 2008 global financial crisis. Although initially focused largely on energy and transport infrastructure, PPPs have increasingly moved into the provision of 'social infrastructure', such as schools, hospitals and healthcare services. Much of the growth of PPPs has been in middle-income countries (MICs) and in two regions, Latin America and the Caribbean, and East Asia and Pacific.

PPPs are a flagship policy of the World Bank, which views them as 'critical' to achieving its development goals. Lending for PPPs has increased three-fold over the past ten years. Over the period 2002–12, the bank's private sector arm, the International Finance Corporation (IFC), invested $6.2 billion in 176 PPPs. In addition, $5.1 billion was provided in insurance cover for 81 PPP projects through the bank's Multilateral Investment Guarantee Agency (MIGA). World Bank funding has played a major role in creating 'an enabling environment' for PPPs. Under the bank's tutelage, numerous developing countries have now introduced legislation to allow PPPs – indeed, a country's deemed 'investment risk' (and to an extent credit rating) is in part determined by the 'quality' of the legislation it has put in place.

The World Bank claims that PPPs are a mechanism for spreading wealth ('helping to eliminate poverty through private involvement in infrastructure') by bringing private sector discipline to public projects, improving operational efficiency, lowering costs and providing better value for money. But the bank's own Internal Evaluation Group (IEG) has found little evidence to support these claims, which have also been rejected by numerous independent analysts. In 2014 the IEG revealed that, despite years of promoting PPPs, the bank lacked data on their actual long-term performance; projects were not tracked after loans had been fully disbursed; and the main measure that the bank used to judge 'success' is 'business performance'. Incredibly, given the bank's mandate to relieve poverty, the IEG was unable to assess 'how far PPPs benefited the poor, as large data gaps exist'. The claimed success rates for PPPs are also highly misleading, in that the evaluations bundle together different criteria, with the result that very poor performances for equity and affordability are obscured by the purported success of other criteria such as 'efficiency'.

Critics argue that the bank's ideologically driven promotion of PPPs is less about financing development (which is at best a sideshow) than about developing finance.

Sources: Hall 2015; Romero 2015; World Bank 2014a

in using PPPs to milk public income streams. For the defining (if rarely stated) feature of PPPs is the government-backed guarantees that they provide investors. As such, they constitute what finance (if not the rest of us) defines as 'infrastructure': and it is this that makes them a cornerstone for transforming infrastructure into an asset class capable of providing yield-hungry investors with the returns that they seek. Like the rapscallion thief in the parody of Oliver Goldsmith's eighteenth-century poem *The Village Blacksmith*, investors have engineered a raft of schemes to ensure that for every penny they put into the public plate, several public pennies are taken out. One difference, however, is that no 'conscience-stricken tear' need be shed: such extraction is not just normalised but encouraged, even at the expense of some of the poorest people in the world.

3.4 Stand and deliver

The guarantees typically embedded in PPP contracts reflect the power of the private sector to dictate terms. Heavily lawyered-up, investors have succeeded in securing guaranteed rates of return; minimum guaranteed income streams; guarantees on loan repayments; guarantees against currency exchange rate risks; guaranteed minimum service charge payments, irrespective of the performance of the PPP; and guarantees of compensation should new legislation affect the profitability of their investments. To give some examples:

● *Guaranteed profits*
Guaranteed rates of return – which, to be clear, mean that the investors make a profit regardless of performance – are a feature of many PPP contracts. An infamous example, whose clauses were so controversial that they sparked an insurrection, is the concession agreement signed in 1999 by the Bolivian government for the running of the water supply system in the city of Cochabamba. The contract with a consortium called Aguas del Tunari (controlled by a UK engineering firm that was then wholly owned by the US multinational Bechtel) guaranteed the company a minimum 15 per cent return on its investment in every year of the 40-year concession.[3] In another example, subsidiaries of water multinationals Thames Water and Suez reportedly negotiated a concession agreement in Indonesia under which the public authorities covered all the companies' costs, including investment, and guaranteed 'a return on capital of 22 per cent' (Hall 2015). In Chile, road concessionaires typically do not have to share revenues with the government until their takings are sufficient to yield a 15 per cent rate of return on invested capital. Meanwhile, the UK Association of Certified Chartered Accountants reports that, during the 1990s, most foreign investors in China 'would usually request a guarantee of a fixed or even minimum return' (ACCA 2012), although the excessive rates demanded by the investors have on occasion led to licences being challenged. A case in point is the Da Chang BOT-built water treatment plant, which RWE Thames Water exited after the Chinese government declared that the municipal guarantee of a 16 per cent profit was invalid since it exceeded the recommended guaranteed return of 8–12 per cent, which is low by international standards.

● *Minimum Revenue Guarantees*
Minimum Revenue Guarantees (MRGs) bind governments to paying the difference if a concession's revenues are lower than those that have been pre-defined in a PPP contract. MRGs have been widely used as a form of guarantee for PPPs in Latin America, South Africa and Malaysia, particularly for airports, ports, toll roads and public transport concessions.

Examples from Latin America include $27 million worth of guarantees agreed by Peru's Investment Promotion Agency (Proinversion) for a container port concession at Paita; $225 million in guarantees agreed for Colombia's El Dorado airport's second runway; and a

Puerto Rican toll bridge where the government agreed to buy back the concession if traffic fell short of its predicted flow, in addition to paying the concessionaire for all project costs and a 13 per cent return on its investment. Mexico also recently guaranteed minimum payments to a concession for running two prisons. As of 2012, Chile alone has agreed to a total of $7 billion worth of MRGs, which have been described as 'the first and most important instrument for attracting investors' (Lorenzen *et al*. 2001, p. 15).

In Asia, Korea guarantees 75 per cent of projected revenue for ten years of a concession. Previously the guarantees covered 70–90 per cent of the projected revenue for fifteen years. In one case, a toll road linking Seoul to a new airport at Incheon outside the South Korean capital, the government had to pay tens of millions of dollars every year when traffic forecasts proved lower than expected, costing an estimated $1.5 billion over the entire length of the concession.

● *Take or Pay contracts*
Take or Pay contracts are contracts between a buyer and a seller under which the buyer is unconditionally obliged to pay for contracted goods or services regardless of whether or not they are delivered or taken. First developed in the energy sector, they are now a feature of PPP contracts in many fields, despite being of questionable legality. With PPPs, such agreements are usually backed by a government guarantee: if the buyer fails to honour the contract, the government steps in to make the payments. An example from the water sector is the Yuvacik Dam near Izmit in Turkey, which was constructed by Thames Water under a BOT agreement. The contract stipulated that the water would be purchased at an agreed price by specified industrial users and neighbouring municipalities. However, the water proved very expensive and the contracted buyers refused to buy, leaving the Turkish government paying 'over the odds for water which is too expensive for its intended customers' (Hall and Lobina 2006).

In the energy sector, Take or Pay contracts in the form of Power Purchasing Agreements (PPAs) similarly bind power distributors, usually state-owned entities, to buy the power from a PPP power generator, often at inflated prices. The PPA for the controversial Nam Theun 2 Hydropower Project in Laos – the world's largest private sector cross-border power project – binds EGAT, the state-owned Thai electricity generating company, to buying electricity at a price higher than that offered by other available sources in Thailand, which already has a surplus of generating capacity. In the Philippines, a Take or Pay contract between the state power utility, Napocor, and Keilco, a Korean company that was developing a gas-fired plant, was one of several contracts that resulted in Napocor running out of money and the government having to take over its debts.

● *Availability payments*
Here the government undertakes to pay the concessionaire a fee based on the availability of the infrastructure asset once it has been constructed. These payments must be made even if the asset is not actually being used, creating income streams that are effectively insulated from competition.

As a result of such contracts, some local authorities are now paying for projects that have never actually been used by the general public or that have closed due to low demand. These include a number of airports and railway stations in Spain and a high school in Northern Ireland. Like Minimum Payment Guarantees, availability contracts drastically curtail the future options of public authorities when it comes to infrastructure planning and development. Locked into contracts that oblige payments for a given project, the pressure is on to make sure that the project is used, even if that means competing projects that might serve the public better are allowed to deteriorate. Indeed, the contracts may actually oblige such neglect in order to ensure the use of the PPP. An example is a contract provision for a PPP toll road in California that forbade the state government from performing repairs and upkeep on the parallel, public, non-tolled lanes. For PPPs in developing countries, the World Bank (2015c) specifically recommends contractual clauses that oblige governments to compensate the project developers where 'similar infrastructure' is constructed that undermines the PPP's financial viability. So, just to be clear, the World Bank recommends penalising, say, Lesotho if it were to build a new hospital that took 'trade' away from the PPP-financed Queen 'Mamohato Memorial Hospital. No doubt, then, as to whose side the bank is on.

● *Loan guarantees*
PPPs are typically wrapped in multiple guarantees that bind governments to servicing project loans if the private sector partner

fails to do so. Obtaining such guarantees is usually a pre-condition set by banks before they will agree to lend developers the money for their project. In some cases, the guarantees come in the form of blanket protection against the risk of a PPP company's default on loan repayment or its bankruptcy, irrespective of the reasons for such failure. PPP contracts recently developed in Turkey, for instance, contain clauses committing the government to taking on the private partner's debts in the event of a default. In the UK, too, some PPP contracts have 'virtually guaranteed' full payment of senior debt,[4] even when a project is terminated because of 'contractor default'. Likewise, a build–lease–transfer urban metro project in the Philippines included a debt-service guarantee that ensured the project could repay its lenders 'come hell or high water' (Irwin 2007, p. 3). The contract also guaranteed investors a 15 per cent return on their shares. In South Africa, loan guarantees have proved 'crucial' to implementing PPP toll-road projects: equity partners were willing to invest only if such guarantees were available.

Even where there are no explicit loan guarantees, the state often has little option but to bail out projects in the event of a PPP's failure (that is, its failure from the public's point of view; finance always seems to walk off carefree into the sunset). In Mexico, for example, an ambitious road-building scheme involving more than 50 concessions ran into difficulties in the 1990s. The concessionaires had borrowed heavily from local state banks. When they failed to repay the loans, the federal government stepped in, assuming some $7.7 billion in debt even though no explicit guarantees were in place. The UK government similarly bailed out Transport for London, a public body which had guaranteed 95 per cent of the debt for a contract with Metronet to upgrade the London Underground under Britain's Private Finance Initiative (PFI), the UK's version of a PPP. When the deal fell apart, the Department for Transport was forced to make a £1.7 billion payment to Transport for London to meet the guarantee. Taxpayers eventually took the hit, incurring a direct loss of between £170 million and £410 million.

New forms of loan guarantees are constantly being developed. Recently, for example, the European Investment Bank (EIB), a public bank, introduced a scheme to guarantee the repayment of loans raised not from banks but through so-called project bonds – tradeable IOUs that are sold to investors to finance specific projects. Such bonds, which offer impressive returns (11 per cent on one solar project in South Africa), are increasingly used in the US, Europe, Latin America and a number of African countries to raise finance for projects, accounting for 13 per cent of the total project finance raised in 2013. Peru recently issued its largest ever project bond for a power transmission line between Lima and the southwest of the country. Under the EIB's scheme, repayments to senior project bond holders would be ensured through a loan or guarantee from the EIB to the project company. The facility, which has been criticised by civil society groups as corporate welfare, guarantees 'all project-related risks affecting the cash flow generation from the start of the operating period, as well as any funding shortfall during the construction period' (European Commission 2015a).

- *Financial and economic equilibrium clauses*

  Financial and economic equilibrium (FEC) clauses, also known as 'stabilisation' or 'adverse action' clauses, entitle the private company to compensation for changes in laws or regulations that adversely affect a project's revenues or its market value. They are a common feature of PPPs in many jurisdictions – indeed the World Bank (2015c) specifically recommends their inclusion in contracts. In the Philippines, which is seeking to attract $10 billion a year from private sector infrastructure investors, all infrastructure projects built on a PPP basis are now guaranteed against 'regulatory risk'. In Indonesia, the government has similarly set up a fund to compensate investors who 'lose out' from 'unpredictable government policy changes' (*Infrastructure Investor* 2010). Indeed, governments have few other choices if they are to attract private sector investors into infrastructure. Concessionaires surveyed by the World Bank in Brazil were explicit that they would not even consider participating in or financing a PPP unless such clauses were included. In Colombia, too, interviewees stated that 'FEC was essential for project financing' (World Bank Institute 2012).

  Stabilisation clauses in PPPs have been successfully invoked in Brazil to win compensation for exchange rate losses when the government changed its currency exchange policy in 1999, and by bus service concessionaires to challenge a law that exempted senior citizens from paying fares. In the US, adverse action clauses have similarly been used to ensure compensation for toll road operators affected by carpooling (the sharing of vehicles), a measure that many states encourage to reduce congestion and environmental pollution.

Even when stabilisation clauses have not been explicitly written into contracts, private companies are able to achieve the same ends through clauses in Bilateral Investment Treaties (BITs) that protect them against the nationalisation or expropriation of businesses. In 2003, for example, a consortium of foreign investors, including multinational companies Suez, Vivendi and Anglian Water, sued the Government of Argentina after it froze water tariffs and devalued the Argentinian peso in response to an economic crisis. The investors, whose subsidiaries held water concessions in Buenos Aires, argued that Argentina's actions violated the 'fair and equitable treatment' protections contained in BITs signed by Argentina with the investors' home countries. Argentina countered that its actions stemmed from its overriding obligation, under international human rights law, to protect its citizens' right to water. Argentina lost the case and was ordered by the International Centre for Settlement of Investment Disputes to pay $405 million to the companies (ICSID 2010).

Stabilisation clauses have been criticised by the UN High Commissioner on Human Rights (2003) for their 'chilling effect' in discouraging governments from passing social and environmental legislation, for which they may have to pay the companies' lost revenues. Indeed, by giving concessionaires contractual rights to subvert or block the introduction of new laws and regulations that protect the public, they effectively 'elevate private contractors to a quasi-governmental status' (Dannin 2011, p. 72). The contracts not only lock in profits but also lock out democracy, giving private parties a disproportionate influence (enforceable via the courts) over which laws get passed and which do not. BIT by BIT, PPP contract by PPP contract, stabilisation clauses privatise policy and the law by establishing a regime of investor rights that effectively bypass, supersede or dismantle public interest legislation, placing investors above governments and citizens (Hildyard and Muttitt 2006).

3.5 Liens on the state

The above list of guarantees found in PPP contracts is by no means exhaustive; others exist and new ones are being developed all the time. David Hall, whose work at the Public Services International Research Unit at the University of Greenwich has been at the forefront of exposing the subsidies involved, puts their financial value to the private sector at $100 billion (Hall 2015).

Each guarantee further locks in the trajectory of privatisation: taking privatised public services back into public ownership incurs stiff financial penalties that act as a deterrent to renationalisation. Each restricts a government's ability to invest itself: PPP payments eat up health, transport and energy budgets, leaving governments with little room for manoeuvre (in the case of Portugal, 'the annual payments to just two major road PPPs cost €800 million, larger than the entire national transport budget of €700 million' (Hall 2015, n.p.)). And each adds to the burgeoning off-balance-sheet liabilities that countries have incurred through PPPs, storing up debt crises for future generations – Portugal alone has clocked up PPP liabilities equivalent to 5 per cent of GDP, while Peru's were estimated at $6.5 billion in 2012.

But, from finance's point of view, the guarantees are a crock of gold, providing legally enforceable liens on future public flows of money that are irrevocable for the length of the contract. Once signed, they cannot be withdrawn, unlike tax breaks and other subsidies which remain at a government's discretion. And because the underlying contracts enjoy the full backing of a sovereign guarantee, they provide building blocks for engineering further contracted income streams that expand infrastructure as an asset class. For example, guaranteed PPP bank loans, which enjoy a high credit rating, are regularly bundled together and the rights to their future repayments sold on to investors seeking more distanced exposure to 'infrastructure', a process known as 'securitisation', whose systemic risks came home to roost when US homeowners defaulted on similarly bundled up mortgage repayments, triggering the financial crisis of 2008.[5]

Such loan securitisations, once exclusively the financial playground of US and European bankers, are becoming more common in developing countries as African, Asian and Latin American capital markets become more sophisticated. Other guaranteed income streams, such as the future revenues from toll payments or cash subsidies received for projects from governments, can be similarly securitised, creating a new strata of investible 'infrastructure' and new vehicles to deliver it to investors. Nor is it just private sector finance that is playing the infrastructure securitisation game: to raise funds to guarantee PPP projects, several municipalities in Mexico have securitised future local tax collections.

The result is a web of contracted income streams, some directly guaranteed, others indirectly guaranteed, that provide multiple avenues through which investors can now extract wealth through 'infrastructure'. Most do not involve direct investment in new projects: by far the majority are in so-called 'brownfield sites' (that is, existing facilities) or in financial products that have been constructed at a secondary level. Critically, the vast majority would not even be available were it not for the privatisation (in all its forms) of infrastructure. And even though the state remains the major financier and operator of public services, the relatively small space that has now been opened up by private investors has enabled finance to construct a multi-billion-dollar extraction machine, with major ramifications for inequality. It is to the workings of this extraction machine that we now turn.

Notes

1 During this period, huge swathes of public infrastructure were sold off to private investors as countries around the world adopted (or were forced to adopt through IMF-imposed structural adjustment policies) privatisation programmes. European governments alone have privatised 640 transportation, utility and telecommunication firms, 'cumulatively worth more than $3 trillion' (Rothballer and Kaserer 2012, p. 95). A further $200 billion of state-owned infrastructure assets have been sold in non-OECD countries (Weber and Alfen 2010).

2 In some sectors, such as ports and energy utilities, privatisation proved a money spinner but water and rail proved particularly resistant to delivering the returns that investors sought.

3 The concession was eventually revoked by the Bolivian government after a public uprising during which several people were killed. Bechtel fought back with a $50 million legal suit against Bolivia before a closed-door trade court operated by the World Bank's International Centre for Settlement of Investment Disputes (ICSID). Following an international campaign by citizens' groups, the company, which had sought not only return on its investment but also 'lost future profits', settled the case with no compensation being paid.

4 Senior debt is debt whose repayment takes priority over other debt, generally because it is secured against the collateral of the borrower or otherwise guaranteed.

5 'Securitisation' is a process whereby assets that generate regular streams of income (such as loans, corporate bonds, mortgages, export credit debt, care homes, gas pipeline contracts or even music rights on songs by rock stars like David Bowie) are sold to a newly created company, a Special Purpose Vehicle (SPV). The SPV then issues derivatives that give investors the right to the income stream from the assets (Hildyard 2008).

Chapter 4

Extraction in motion: infrastructure-as-asset-class

4.1 Yield hogs

For investors, 'infrastructure' is now an 'asset class',[1] the boundaries of which are limited only by the ability of finance to build new contracted income streams that extract wealth, directly or indirectly, from the activities that surround the funding, construction and operation of infrastructure facilities. What started off with investments in so-called *economic infrastructure* (utilities, roads, ports, airports and the like) now include investments in *resource/commodity infrastructure* (oil and gas facilities, mining, forests and food storage facilities), *social infrastructure* (hospitals, public housing, schools, prisons, law courts and military bases), *information infrastructure* (cloud-based computing systems and big data harvesting) and, still in its infancy, *natural infrastructure* (where income streams are constructed through payment for so-called environmental services).

Starving for yield, investors are flocking to infrastructure in the belief that it will deliver higher returns than investments in other asset classes. Pension funds, in particular, are attracted by the hope that 'infrastructure' will rescue them from the 'ballooning deficits and widening shortfalls' (Noble and Antonatos 2014) that they have built up as a result of low bond yields and decades of poor investments (Minns and Sexton 2006). In the UK alone, pension schemes now have an aggregate deficit of £367.5 billion, leading many to turn to high-risk 'alternative assets', including infrastructure, in an attempt to bolster their balance sheet and meet their future liabilities, a move that the OECD (2015a) warns could 'seriously compromise' their solvency. Insurance companies, which like pension funds also need to earn minimum absolute returns, are also turning to infrastructure investments, notably the provision of debt. Sovereign Wealth Funds, insurance companies, endowment funds, High Net Worth individuals and a range of other players are similarly pouring money into the 'infrastructure space'. And, as *Infrastructure Investor* records, 'the biggest concern for most investors is how to grab a slice of the emerging market pie' (Thomson 2014b, p. 1).

There are many ways in which investors can invest in infrastructure, depending on their appetite for risk. Generally, such investments take the form of equity or debt: equity refers to financial resources that are provided by investors in return for an ownership interest in an asset; debt refers to money lent by investors, either as bank loans or through the purchase of tradeable IOUs such as bonds. For investors, the highest returns – and the riskiest investments – come from financing new projects, known as 'greenfield' investments. Some of these greenfield projects are Public–Private Partnerships but many are not; oil, gas, coal and mining companies, for example, regularly finance roads, railways, ports, power plants, pipelines and water facilities as part of a specific resource-extraction project, without entering into a PPP. Less risky are 'brownfield' projects: facilities that have already been built but that are being privatised or opened up to PPP management contracts. But much of the $3 trillion plus that is invested by private investors in infrastructure is one step or more removed from direct holdings in actual bricks and mortar. Instead the investments are in the parent companies that are developing projects (rather than the subsidiaries that build them) or in companies that stand to benefit from infrastructure contracts, for example, construction and engineering companies, designers and equipment suppliers. Here the money is made primarily through building up order books rather than investing in actual projects.

Most investors have traditionally invested through buying shares in infrastructure companies listed on stock exchanges or buying fixed-income instruments, such as corporate bonds. This remains the main route through which institutional investors gain exposure to infrastructure. Canadian pension funds, for example, have recently invested directly in water and energy distribution companies, toll roads in Chile and a gas pipeline in Peru. Insurance companies are similarly making increased direct investments in infrastructure debt.

But, as detailed below, finance now provides a range of intermediary vehicles through which investors can invest at a distance in infrastructure companies and projects, without the higher risks of direct ownership. Most of these vehicles involve some form of pooled fund, which is managed on behalf of the investor by a fund manager, such as investment bank Goldman Sachs (infamously branded the 'Vampire Squid' by *Rolling Stone* magazine (Taibbi 2010)). The most commonly used pooled funds include Exchange Traded Funds (ETFs), infrastructure funds, infrastructure funds-of-funds, infrastructure debt funds, venture capital and private equity funds, and hedge funds (OECD 2015b). A World Bank study found that private equity funds are the main infrastructure investment vehicles for pension funds in Brazil, Colombia, Peru and Mexico, while direct purchases of infrastructure bonds are popular in Chile and South Africa (Inderst and Stewart 2014).

4.2 Extraction strategies and vehicles

The different vehicles allow different investment strategies, with different yields and rates of return. Investors seeking liquid (that is, relatively easily disposable) exposure to 'infrastructure', for example, might chose an actively managed index fund[2] or an Exchange Traded Fund (ETF).[3] Infrastructure ETFs in the US had more than $10 billion in assets in 2014, with one energy-focused fund, Energy MLP ETF, gathering an estimated $326 million per month in net inflows between 2011 and 2014. A number of funds track infrastructure in Asia, such as the HSBC MSCI Indonesia ETF and the MSCI Philippines TRN Index ETF. The yields are typically of the order of 2–3 per cent. Exchange Traded Funds have the added attraction for some institutional investors of providing access to areas of the infrastructure market that 'previously might have been less-accessible or even prohibited' (Russell Investments 2014).

More hands-on investment vehicles, like dedicated infrastructure funds, allow for other strategies. Most have, historically, tended to avoid direct investments in greenfield projects (although these do occur), since the contracted income streams they seek come into play only once a project is up and running. Instead, the investments tend to be in brownfield projects, including PPPs. Dedicated infrastructure funds, which invest in both equity and debt, are the most favoured vehicles for institutional investors seeking to build exposure to infrastructure. More than 450 such funds exist, overseen by about 270 management companies, and their number is increasing. Between 2002 and 2012 they raised an estimated $214 billion for investment, mostly in the US and Europe but also, increasingly, in emerging markets. In 2012, for example, funds aimed at Asia, Latin America and other emerging market countries accounted for 37 per cent of the monies raised. Although marketed as providing steady, long-term income from contracted infrastructure income streams, many of the projects in which they are invested are highly leveraged (that is, their borrowings are significantly higher than the value of their shares or 'equity'), adding considerably to their investment risk, an issue of concern given the increasing investments by pension funds on which workers rely for their retirement.

Most dedicated infrastructure funds have focused historically on Europe and the US, generating returns in the mid-teens (although, prior to the financial crisis, Macquarie, one of the biggest fund managers, boasted enviable average returns of 19.8 per cent). However, there is growing interest from Western investors in infrastructure and funds that have been established within developing countries. Funds that have invested in Asia, Latin America or Africa include the JPMorgan Asian Infrastructure and Related Resources Opportunity Fund II; the Macquarie Infrastructure and Real Asset's LAC-China Infrastructure Fund; the Abraaj Infrastructure and Growth Capital Fund; Actis's Infrastructure Fund II; Brookfield Asset Management's Transelec Transmission; and the Morgan Stanley Infrastructure Partners II fund (Hildyard 2012). Debt funds – that is, funds that raise money from investors to lend to infrastructure companies or projects – are also focusing on developing countries. As of January 2015, 31 unlisted infrastructure debt funds were 'on the road', that is, seeking to raise money from investors. Among the biggest were the Global Infrastructure Partners Capital Solutions Fund, launched by Global Infrastructure Partners, with a fund-raising target of $2.5 billion, and two Indian funds, the IL&FS Infrastructure Debt Fund and the IIFCL Infrastructure Debt Fund (Preqin 2015).

India, China and Indonesia are currently identified as 'the most attractive candidates for infrastructure investing', but, for the savvy investor, the entire Asia region is said to offer 'attractive opportunities' (Hudgins and Sharma 2014). Returns are high. By targeting the most attractive infrastructure sub-sectors within each country market – power, renewable energy, logistics, roads and railways in the Philippines, for example, as against power, oil and gas and roads in Malaysia – JPMorgan reportedly expects returns in the 'high teens' (Hudgins and Sharma 2014). To put that into perspective, at a 15 per cent annual rate of return, a $1 billion fund would expect to return $1.5 billion in profit to investors (on top of the original investment) over its ten-year life. Nice work if you can get it.

Other funds – notably private equity and venture capital funds – offer still higher returns. Unlike infrastructure funds, their approach is opportunistic and riskier. Instead of building a portfolio dedicated to infrastructure investments, they invest in infrastructure as and when prospects emerge. Generally, the strategy is to create value by building up a company's portfolio of contracted revenues and 'improving' its business model (yes, business models are considered part of 'infrastructure'). The investment is then 'flipped' either through a private sale or by taking the company public through a stock market listing. Minimum expected returns for funds involved in this type of investment in emerging markets are typically 20–25 per cent. However, this figure reflects the return of the fund's overall portfolio and thus hides both the much higher returns (300 per cent is not untypical) that are often made on some individual investments and the large losses made on others. With banks increasingly withdrawing from project finance as they seek to rebuild their balance sheets in the wake of the 2008 financial crisis, private equity funds are now offering debt finance as well as equity. Indeed, rating agency Standard & Poor's predicts that they will soon take over as the major providers of infrastructure debt (S&P Capital IQ 2015). Debt providers expect a minimum 10 per cent rate of return for projects in Africa, which compares favourably with the 4–5 per cent yields available on sovereign debt of the same credit rating.

The different investment vehicles also offer different investment strategies. One fund may invest in mature assets with solid contracted cash flows. Another may pick a portfolio composed entirely of assets in the development phase where the contracted cash flows are still 'under construction'. Specialist venture capital funds, for example, may seek to profit by investing at an early stage in a project with a view to 'anaesthetising the risks that infrastructure investors don't like', as Tony Mallin of Star Capital, a London-based fund, puts it, and transforming a project 'into something that looks like infrastructure' (Thomson 2014a). Different funds employ different means of doing this but strategies have included securing government guarantees, negotiating favourable off-take contracts or creating new income streams, such as carbon credits, which will increase the value of the asset to later-stage investors. Tax and regulatory exemptions may also be sought, along with non-competition clauses.

As a project nears completion, so-called 'final mile' investors enter the fray, seeking to ramp up income streams before selling the investment back to the market once the project is up and running, a strategy that JPMorgan reportedly intends to employ in emerging markets in Asia (Kranc 2014). Historically, such 'ramping up' has involved enforcing non-competition clauses; introducing industrial-style management techniques to reduce the 'average length of stay' – ALOS in the jargon – of patients in hospitals to ensure maximum bed occupation; weeding out customers who cannot afford to pay user fees; and, in the case of one US higher education provider, recruiting students to online courses, regardless of whether they are qualified or not, through what are alleged to have been aggressive call centre sales techniques (UCU 2012).

Further opportunities for profit come after a project is completed – and not just through operating the constructed infrastructure. Schools, hospitals, railways and roads are now tradeable commodities. In recent years, for example, a booming worldwide secondary market has mushroomed in the sale of equity in completed PPP project companies, earning investors an average rate of return of 29 per cent. This is twice the 12–15 per cent rate of return that was typically predicted when the contracts for the project were signed, yet the public sector partner receives none of the profits from the sale. Dexter Whitfield (2014) of the European Services Strategy Unit (ESSU) calculates that the extra profit extracted through secondary market sales of PPPs in the UK could be as high as £2.65 billion. In Latin America, where a secondary market in PPPs is well established, the Swedish construction company Skanska made an average profit of 52 per cent from four secondary market sales, including $350 million on one toll road in Chile and $45 million on the Ponte de Pedra hydroelectric project in Brazil.

But the financial extraction does not end here.

4.3 Fee factories

The day-to-day operations of the funds themselves and the 'infrastructure' in which they invest have now become platforms from which satellite 'profit points' are constructed, Meccano-like, through elaborate forms of financial engineering. A hotchpotch of acronym-laden financial products – from CDOs (collaterised debt obligations)[4] to CDSs (credit default swaps)[5] – come into play as investors seek to squeeze further profit from their investments by securitising income streams or by parcelling off risks. Raising the finance to build a privately financed power plant, for example, no longer involves (as it did in the past) going to a bank (or even a group of banks) and seeking a loan, which then remains on the bank's books until it is repaid. Instead the loan is distributed via what the New York Federal Reserve has called 'a daisy-chain of non-bank financial intermediaries' (Pozsar *et al.* 2012, p. 10), each taking their cut at each step in the process. Securitisation, too, has been extended beyond packaging up bank loans to a whole range of infrastructure-related income streams. Some privately owned utilities, for example, have securitised future income streams from customers, using the proceeds to increase dividends to shareholders, as the UK's Thames Water did in 2007 (Allen and Pryke

2013; Bayliss 2014). The practice has led journalist James Meek to comment that the bill-paying public is effectively being packaged up and 'sold, sector by sector, to investors' (Meek 2012).

The result is a bewilderingly cat's cradle of financial products, with each additional transaction generating opportunities for speculation by intermediaries and arrangement fees for a cluster of professions – from lawyers to accountants, consultancies and tax advisers. The UK Association of Certified Chartered Accountants estimates that fees to 'third party advisers' accounted for 2.6 per cent of project costs for UK PFI deals closed between 2004 and 2006 (ACCA 2012). Most of the advisors were from the 'Big Four' accountancy firms – PWC, Deloitte, KPMG and Ernst & Young (Shaoul *et al.* 2006; Hall 2015). In total, consultants and lawyers walked away with over £400 million in fees from the failed attempt to introduce PPPs for the London Underground. The *Financial Times* calculates that, by 2011, they had earned at least £2.8 billion and probably well over £4 billion advising on PFI deals (Timmins and Giles 2011). UK law firms that have strong PFI practices include Allen & Overy, Clifford Chance, Linklaters and Norton Rose Fulbright.

Infrastructure has also become a 'fee factory' for the banks, particularly those that run their own funds, such as Macquarie Bank. In 2007 *Fortune* magazine revealed that Macquarie Infrastructure Group (MIG), at the time Macquarie's largest infrastructure fund, paid Macquarie Bank a total of almost A$150 million in banking fees and another A$273 million in management fees. In some cases, fees were generated by one Macquarie fund buying assets off another Macquarie fund. In 2006, for example, a fund called Macquarie Infrastructure Partners (MIP) bought 50 per cent of MIG's interest in four toll roads for $825 million, 'resulting in roughly a $175 million profit to MIG (and A$5.8 million in fees to Macquarie Bank)' (McLean 2007).

4.4 Many happy returns (for the 1%)

Promoters of PPPs – from the World Bank, the Asian Development Bank, the European Investment Bank, World Economic Forum, the OECD, the G8 and G20, and a range of policy think tanks – are keen to let us know how much private money is currently being invested in infrastructure, and how much more is needed. But they are mute on the profits that are being made from these investments. Not one of them has published even a ball park figure. Such data as exists is widely scattered, fragmented and generally available only at a price.

Specialist magazines, such as *Infrastructure Investor*, carry interviews with fund managers who allude to the returns they hope to make from their investments. Companies such as Preqin collect and publish comprehensive data on the infrastructure and private equity funds currently investing or raising funds to invest. Independent researchers, such as Dexter Whitfield, have patiently combed the published accounts of infrastructure companies to compile a database of returns from secondary market sales of PPP projects. And, occasionally, fund managers give details of the returns they have made. Actis, a private equity fund-of-funds formed in 2004 following the restructuring of the Commonwealth Development Corporation (CDC),[6] the UK's publicly financed development finance institution, has revealed that it has made $2.2 billion from the $867 million it has invested in infrastructure since 2004 (Thomson 2015). That is a rate of return of more than 250 per cent from investments that have, in several cases, been widely criticised for involving massive hikes in the prices charged to consumers to the detriment of poorer people.

By and large, however, there is precious little information available on the actual performance of investments. For the most part, funds like to keep that information to themselves. However, some academic research is available (Peng and Newell 2007), which, together with reports from within the financial industry itself, give an indication of the range of returns for different infrastructure investments (see Exhibit 4.1). The figures need to be taken with a large pinch of salt, not least because the reporting by many fund managers is widely viewed as 'both inaccurate and inadequate' (Blanc-Brude 2014, p. 15). In addition, the estimates are derived from a limited number of investments, many made prior to the 2008 global financial crisis, and over a limited period. Returns also vary widely from market to market and sector to sector, so averages can be misleading. Moreover, the same physical asset can deliver a range of returns depending on the stage at which an investment takes place and the way in which a deal is structured.

But, despite these caveats, the figures make it possible to piece together a partial picture of the amounts extracted annually, at least from developing countries. For 2014 the World Bank (2015a) records $100.7 billion of private investment in developing countries: $28.5 billion of it in roads, $16.4 billion in airports and seaports, $10.4 billion in railways and $45.4 billion in electricity projects (see Exhibit 4.1). Reported annual rates of return for toll road projects range between 8 per cent and 26 per cent (Inderst 2010; Weber and Alfen 2010): so at 8 per cent, the investors in road projects would

Exhibit 4.1 Reported returns by infrastructure asset type and estimates of extraction

Asset	Range of reported annual returns	Amount invested in 2014 in developing countries	Likely extraction over standard 25-year concession period
Toll roads	8–26%	$28.5 bn	$57 bn–$185.25 bn
Airports / seaports	8–8%	$16.4 bn	$32.8 bn–$73.8 bn
Railways	14–18%	$10.4 bn*	$36.4 bn–$46.8 bn
Electricity	15–25%	$45.4 bn	$170.25 bn–$283.75 bn
TOTAL		**$100.7 bn**	**$296.45– $589.6 bn**

Sources: Inderst 2010; JPMorgan Asset Management 2010; Peng and Newell 2007; Whitfield 2014; Weber and Alfen 2010; World Bank 2015a

*The World Bank does not give an aggregate figure for rail investment. However, the figure can be derived by subtracting cited totals in World Bank (2015a) for roads, airports/seaports from the total of all transport investments ($55.3 bn) in the sectors covered.

stand to make just over $2 billion a year; at 26 per cent, their annual return would be close to $7.5 billion. Over the 25 years that the concessions are likely to last, the total extracted from toll roads would be between $57 billion and $185 billion. For airports and ports, where reported returns are 8–18 per cent, the comparable figures would be $1.3 billion to nearly $3 billion a year, giving a total of somewhere between $33 billion and $74 billion over a 25-year concession period. Rail typically makes returns of 14–18 per cent, yielding an annual $1.4 billion to nearly $2 billion, suggesting some $36 billion to $47 billion over the concession period. Electricity projects, with typical annual returns of 15–25 per cent, would return to investors in one year anything between $7 billion to over $11 billion, amounting to $170 billion to $284 billion over 25 years. All told, the $100.7 billion invested in the energy, water and transport sectors in 2014 in developing countries would probably return to investors somewhere between $296 billion and nearly $590 billion over 25 years *on top of* their original investments (see Exhibit 4.1).

Performing a similar exercise for the estimated $600–700 billion invested annually in dedicated infrastructure funds by institutional investors (see Chapter 3) gives another, more global, snapshot of the extent of accumulation-through-infrastructure. According to Preqin, such funds typically target a net return of 15.8 per cent on average (12 per cent for developed markets and 19.3 per cent for emerging markets) (Inderst 2010), although, for Africa, the expected returns can be far higher at 30 per cent. So, if the average return were achieved, and assuming the lower figure of $600 billion was invested, investors would be making $94.8 billion a year or $948 billion over ten years, the lifetime of most unlisted funds. And then there are the returns from the shares in infrastructure companies that are purchased directly (rather than through funds) by investors: the stock market value of these amount to at least $3 trillion (RREEF 2011; Inderst 2010, 2013, 2014). With infrastructure stocks typically yielding 6 per cent a year, such direct equity investments could be returning some $180 billion a year.

On the basis of such back-of-the-envelope calculations, it would thus appear that considerably more is extracted every year through 'infrastructure' than the $100.7 billion directly invested by the private sector in actual projects – perhaps more than twice as much. The main beneficiaries are investors in the developed world, who hold nearly 80 per cent of the world's financial assets. And among this privileged group, it is fund managers who probably stand to benefit most, typically demanding 2 per cent of the money raised for the fund from investors, in addition to 20 per cent of the profits that the fund makes. For a manager of a $1 billion infrastructure fund, that could translate into $320 million, assuming a 150 per cent rate of return over the ten-year lifetime of a typical fund. Small wonder that Macquarie, a major infrastructure fund management firm, has earned the reputation of being 'the millionaires factory' (McLean 2007). For poorer people, however, the cost is higher (often unaffordable) tariffs as infrastructure finance shifts from a system supported by general taxation (where the rich are obliged to help the poor) to one where 'the less well-off enable services, like a road network, that the rich get for what is, to them, a trifling sum' (Meek 2012).

4.5 More guarantees, please

The trajectory is not only towards increased inequality: it is also profoundly undemocratic, elitist – and unstable. Undemocratic because, as infrastructure finance, including state-financed infrastructure, moves increasingly towards raising funds on capital markets, it is a handful of fund managers and rich investors who determine what gets financed and what does not. Elitist because the facilities that would most benefit the poor do not get built; as a report by the NEPAD-OECD Africa Investment Initiative candidly admits, it is 'futile' (their word, not mine) to seek private investors for, say, rural electrification projects 'due to the low returns on investment' (Muzenda 2009, p. 45). And unstable because infrastructure-as-asset-class has become an inflated bubble – and many in finance now warn that the bubble is about to burst.

To expand, as it must, finance's infrastructure relies on a constant stream of contracted income flows coming to the market. But with demand for 'infrastructure' growing among investors – encouraged by the easing of restrictions on pension fund investments (see Box 4.1 'The global pensions grab') – too much money is now chasing too few suitable income streams. The problem is compounded by the reluctance of private investors to finance the construction of new projects. Cost overruns, construction delays, longer than expected demand, ramp-up periods and lower-than-predicted revenues all

Box 4.1 The global pensions grab

Worldwide, governments are looking to the estimated $32 trillion held by pension funds to bridge the so-called 'infrastructure financing gap'. Pension funds, many of which are experiencing difficulties in meeting their future liabilities, are willing partners but, in many countries, are prevented from investing in riskier financial assets, such as infrastructure projects, and have typically invested in safer government bonds.

These restrictions are now being torn up as part of a worldwide 'pensions grab'. In Africa, where pension funds have an estimated $380 billion under management, South Africa, Nigeria and Ghana have rewritten their pension laws, while a number of other countries are planning to do so. Investors predict that the changes in South Africa's legislation could lead to a ten-fold surge in pension fund investments in hedge funds and private equity funds, a high proportion of which (it is expected) will make its way to infrastructure development. In India, controls limiting investments in infrastructure by foreign pension funds have been loosened and further deregulation is expected.

The implications for working people are profound. In countries where pension funds are already allowed to invest in riskier assets, workers have seen their retirement benefits slashed to make up for the massive shortfalls (over $1 trillion in the US) incurred through fund managers having chased high-risk 'alpha' returns. In the US, a study by Dean Baker of the Center for Economic and Policy Research reveals that public sector workers are some $850 billion poorer today as a result of their pensions being invested in stocks and exposed to mortgage-backed securities than they would have been if fund managers had invested in safer Treasury bonds.

Pension fund investments in private equity funds, whose business model often relies on squeezing labour to boost returns, also threaten the interests of workers and undermine solidarity. Although pension holders from one fund may benefit, their fund's investment may cause economic harm to workers elsewhere. As Larry Beeferman of Harvard Law School comments, 'such actions raise the issue of reciprocity and whether the first group can expect support against privatization of their own jobs from workers in locales in which their fund has invested'.

Sources: Baker 2011; Beeferman 2008; European Commission 2015b; Favas 2014; Inderst 2013; OECD 2011; PEI 2011

combine to make profitable financial extraction highly risky. Instead, investors have concentrated on milking income streams from existing facilities. But the flow of such investment opportunities is slowing down, leading to a massive inflation of asset prices, with some assets now selling for more than 25 times their earnings. In the short term, those selling the assets reap high profits; in the longer term, higher prices threaten declining rates of return. Fund managers are reported to be 'desperate' to put the money they have raised to 'work' but are 'finding it difficult to do so without compromising their return targets' (Favas 2015a). Echoes of the mortgage market prior to the 2008 global financial crisis reverberate around the infrastructure space.

Some institutional investors have responded by broadening their investments beyond 'core' income streams from utilities and the like to the riskier outlying frontiers of 'infrastructure' – timber, for instance. Others are looking to create new contracted income streams to boost their revenues through carbon offsets. Still others have simply 'downsized' their infrastructure funds. But the begging bowl is out as finance looks once again to the public to 'combat risk averseness' and 'increase the bankability' of projects (Global Infrastructure Basel 2015). Governments and multilateral development banks have responded by dreaming up yet more schemes to put public money to work for finance's infrastructure. To increase the flow of investible income streams, for example, Australia is proposing further privatisations. But this time around, rather than paying down government debt, a proportion of the proceeds would go to new state-financed infrastructure which, once built, would then (you've guessed it) be privatised, creating a steady flow of investible projects for private investors.

Other governments are extending the PPP structure to financing vehicles. The Philippine government, for example, has set up a public–private fund – the Philippine Investment Alliance for Infrastructure – to provide 'public seed capital' for new private sector infrastructure investment. The cornerstone investors are the Philippine Government Service Insurance System fund (making up half of the fund), the Asian Development Bank and the Dutch pension fund asset manager, APG. The fund is managed by Macquarie. Other similar schemes have been launched by African governments, notably the Pan African Infrastructure Development Fund, whose investors include a mixture of pension funds and public financial institutions such the African Development Bank. Not to be outdone, the World Bank (2014d) has set up the Global Infrastructure Facility (GIF), a public–private initiative funded by governments, multilateral development banks and export credit agencies with the heads of some of the world's largest asset management, private equity, pension and insurance funds, and commercial banks as advisers (among them Macquarie, Partners Group, Blackrock, HSBC and Citibank). The focus of the facility is on preparing projects and making them bankable: that is, profitable for private investors.

The heavy lifting of infrastructure construction will be left to the public sector: afterwards the rich will be invited in, income streams suitably guaranteed, to reap the profits. The words of Thomas Thornton, the frustrated Secretary of Public Works at the India Office in the nineteenth century, echo down the ages: 'private enterprise at public risk'. And sooner or later, the consequences will come home to roost: defaults, bailouts, contagion to other markets as cross-linked derivative trades are called in, and (in the absence of deep-rooted political change) austerity for those who can least afford it. Meanwhile, so long as the music is playing, finance keeps on dancing. Just as it did when the mortgage bubble expanded.

Notes

1 An asset class is a group of securities whose risk profile is held to be uncorrelated to that of other assets.
2 An index fund is a form of mutual fund that seeks to track or outperform a stock market index, such as the S&P BSE India Infrastructure Index, through investments in a basket of selected infrastructure companies.
3 ETFs are similar to index funds but their aim is only to replicate the index rather than outperform it. Unlike index mutual funds, which are priced after a market has closed, ETFs are priced and traded continuously throughout the trading day.
4 A collaterised debt obligation (CDO) is a financial product that is used by banks and other lenders to get loans off their balance sheet. The CDO

pools together cashflow-generating assets, such as mortgages, and repackages them into discrete tranches (reflecting their relative risk) that are then sold to investors. A key feature is that high-risk loans are bundled up with lower risk ones ('sub-prime' mortgages, for example, with 'prime' ones) (Hildyard 2008).

5 A credit default swap (CDS) is a derivative-based financial instrument that provides cover in the event that a loan or a bond defaults. Although often described as 'insurance', CDSs are not insurance in any sense that the mainstream insurance industry would understand, not least because those who do the 'insuring' frequently do not hold a licence and are unregulated under insurance rules. CDSs are better viewed as bets on the creditworthiness of a company (Hildyard 2008).

6 Actis, now an independent company, manages those assets in which CDC had invested prior to its restructuring. In 2012 the total value of the assets managed by Actis was $4.5 billion. Until 2012 the UK's Department for International Development retained a 40 per cent shareholding in Actis, but this shareholding was sold to Actis for £8 million. CDC, however, remains invested in many Actis funds. Actis's 2012 *Review* states: 'CDC Group plc is the anchor investor in each of Actis's funds and represents approximately 45 per cent of total commitments to those funds' (Actis 2012).

Chapter 5

Infrastructure corridors, frontier finance and the vulnerabilities of capital

The instability of infrastructure-as-asset-class and the reluctance of investors to back higher-risk, new, so-called 'greenfield' projects are creating a major problem for the smooth expansion of globalised capital. For infrastructure-as-asset-class is more than just a rent grab by finance or an opportunity for derivative traders to make a quick buck by constructing a superstructure of complex financial trades on the back of state-backed guarantees – though it is certainly both of these things. Its emergence is also an outcome of deeper structural forces that have their roots in a centuries-long trend that has massively increased both the scale and the costs of the physical infrastructure – roads, railways, ports, airports, waterways, energy facilities and the like – that dominant forms of industrial capital need in order to expand.

Multiple social, ecological and political dynamics lie behind this trend; but, from the perspective of understanding the push for greater private sector investment in infrastructure development, one bundle of influential drivers stands out. They stem from a problem that some people in finance now term the 'production–consumption disconnect' (Antropov and Perarnaud 2013). This disconnect arises in part from economies of scale that have enabled more remote deposits of raw materials for industrial production to be extracted; in part from the increasing distances between those deposits and the industrial sites where the extracted resources are transformed into consumer goods; and in part from the distances between those production sites and the places where the 'global consuming class'[1] live.

The problem is not new. Over 150 years ago, Karl Marx revealed how the more that capital expands, the more it needs to improve infrastructure to 'annihilate space by time' (Marx 1858). That reality remains a core challenge for contemporary infrastructure planning within would-be global politburos, such as the World Bank. Marx may not get a mention in the bank's flagship 2009 *World Development* Report *Reshaping Economic Geography* (its takeaway policy summary: 'No country has grown to riches without changing the geographic distribution of its people and production for market access'); but 'annihilating space by time' is *the* leitmotif that runs through the report's 380 pages. Distance is a key theme, defined by the bank not in Euclidean terms but as a measure of time and money – and, more specifically, 'the ease or difficulty for goods, services, labour, capital, information, and ideas to traverse space'. Future profits, the bank insists, will depend on truncating such 'economic distance' not only through better roads, ports and railways but also (true to form) through the removal of tariff barriers. Viewed through this lens, infrastructure becomes 'shorthand for policies and investments that are spatially connective' (World Bank 2009): and the spaces to be connected are the 'sacrifice areas' where resources are extracted and those where industries and richer consumers are sited. The priority is thus to construct a global network of interconnected infrastructure corridors, logistics hubs and new cities aimed at speeding up the circulation of commodities between sites of resource extraction, production and consumption.

As with so many past mega-infrastructure plans (Hildyard and Lohmann 2013), there is an eerie absence of any signs of the social or ecological conflicts that this 'fantasy of universal integration' (Wilson *et al.* 2015b, p. 21) might engender. Glossy PR leaflets show bullet trains streaking across landscapes that are entirely devoid of people; new 'pocket cities' of shimmering glass and steel skyscrapers emerge out of the plains of China without a hint that anyone's life has been blighted through their construction; and the skies over the sleek factories in kilometres-square free trade zones are eternally clear and blue, without a blemish of pollution. On paper – oh! how easily strokes of pen on blank sheets of paper can grant the illusion of omnipotence! – the planned 'spatial connections' drive their way through some of the most hostile and biodiverse terrains on the planet, bulldozing tropical forests, dredging waterways, interconnecting rivers and tunnelling through mountains, seemingly oblivious to the rebelliousness of nature or the resistance of local communities.

Inevitably, the frictionless future portrayed by the global 'annihilators of distance', be they in the World Bank or China's Central Committee, is already bumping up against the realities of protests over land grabs, competing plans by national governments and local businesses, and the sheer intransigence of nature. But beyond these conflicts, the planners' plans are also pressing against the frontiers of traditional infrastructure finance. The money simply isn't available to fund them without tapping a wider pool of finance beyond the state, private banks and multilateral institutions. Global capital markets are the new target source, Public–Private Partnerships the induce-ment, and transforming infrastructure into an asset class the currently favoured means of raising the funds. A failure to entice the sums required from investors thus creates a major additional vulner-ability for capital's corridor programme: and, as such, it has turned infrastructure-as-asset-class into a potent emerging arena of struggle.

How is the 'production–consumption disconnect' playing out today? How critical are the proposed 'spatial connectors' to smooth-ing the onward march of globalisation that policy makers like to project? What do they entail in practice? And how do they relate to the global wealth gap?

5.1 Time, space and infrastructure

While teaching at Oxford University in the 1990s, the Marxist geog-rapher David Harvey used to make a point of asking his first-year students where their last meal came from. It was, he found, a useful way of starting a conversation on the geographies that are obscured by a narrow focus on local physical landscapes. Tracing the meal back beyond the shops where the food had been purchased to the fields where it had been produced and the factories where it had been processed helped to reveal a dependency 'upon a whole world of social labour conducted in many places under very different social relations and conditions of production', exposing the 'fingerprints of exploitation' on the grapes we eat or the green beans we consume. As an exercise, says Harvey, it helped lift the veil on 'the intricate geography of production'. Only when this had been uncovered could the full story of 'the myriad social relationships' that put food upon our tables be told (Harvey 1990, p. 422).

Embedded in that back story, as with other back stories of the many raw materials and goods used in the production of the goods and services we consume, is a long and intricate history of restless innovation, colonialism, intellectual endeavour, brutality, engineer-ing genius, militarism, managerial breakthroughs, trade wars and labour repression as capital has sought to overcome the barriers created by its own expansion. Among such barriers, argues Harvey, those arising from the increased distance between points of produc-tion and points of consumption have proved both perennial and critical. Distance matters because time matters. And time matters because the faster commodities can be produced and exchanged, the greater the profits for individual capitalists and the sharper their competitive edge over rivals.

The struggle to 'annihilate space by time' is thus central to the whole dynamic of capital accumulation (Harvey 2001). Indeed, the history of transportation, communications, logistics and labour is, in many respects, the history of efforts to 'compress time and space' (Harvey 1989) through new technologies and new management practices that enable goods to be moved faster, more cheaply and more efficiently. Improvements in transport and communications – from steamships, canals, railways and the telegraph in the nineteenth century to jet aircraft, containerisation, computerised management systems and satellites in the twentieth – are a large part of this story. But so are the resistances they have provoked from humans and non-humans, and the competitions and collaborations they have spawned between and among national and international governments and firms. Each innovation has made its own historically specific contribution to 'resolve' the irresolvable spatial and temporal tensions that constantly arise as capital expands around the globe in search of the cheapest ways of extracting materials and producing goods. And each in turn has given rise to new spatial and temporal tensions as capital has sought to harness new technologies and their associated political and social infrastructures to bring about economies of scale by reducing still further the unit costs (and time) of transporting raw materials and finished goods from one place to another.

The process is self-reinforcing. To overcome diseconomies of space, bigger, more powerful and more efficient ships, trucks, trains, barges and cargo planes are built. These in turn necessitate expanding or upgrading railway systems and ports; by one reckoning, a new harbour, wharf or terminal can decrease average port costs by 2 per cent, while a new crane reduces port costs by 1 per cent (ADB/ADBI 2009). Roads must be widened, bridges strengthened, canals deepened and widened (the Panama Canal, whose locks are now too small to accommodate larger container ships, is now being upgraded to allow ships that are 25 per cent longer and 50 per cent wider than those it was previously capable of handling), rivers straightened, airport runways lengthened and new warehousing infrastructure constructed to handle the greater throughput of materials. The resulting economies of scale in transport stimulate further economies of scale in production (and vice versa), reducing the costs of raw materials and finished goods, stimulating demand and triggering yet another round of pressures to reduce costs by compressing time and distance. One wave of innovation thus creates pressures for yet further innovation.

As bigger and faster forms of transport are developed and the costs of moving goods fall relative to other costs, the geographies of raw material extraction and production are reconfigured. The choice of location for a factory, for example, no longer rests primarily on its proximity to sources of raw materials or consumers but embraces other considerations such as labour costs, the skills of the available workforce, the local tax regime or the regulatory environment. It becomes more possible for capital to fragment production processes to an unprecedented degree and to move production further and further afield to areas that promise greater profitability, even though these may often be thousands of miles from the major points of consumption. Likewise, remoter sources of raw materials become commercially viable. Until the 1950s, for example, the high costs of transporting iron ore (typically 60 per cent of production costs) meant that steel mills needed to be sited close to the point of iron ore extraction. But by the 1960s developments in shipping had made it competitive for the Japanese steel industry to transport huge volumes of iron ore from Australia over 5,000 miles away. By the 1980s bulk carriers had been developed that were twice the size of anything previously available, enabling Japan to import iron ore from the newly developed Carajas mine in the Brazilian Amazon over 12,000 miles away 'more cheaply than US Steel could ship its iron ore across the Great Lakes' (Bunker and Ciccantell 2005, p. xii).

Today the distances between points of production and points of consumption are often huge, involving multiple journeys and multiple forms of transport. A standard desktop computer, for example, typically involves the assembly of some 4,000 components manufactured by as many as 250 different suppliers whose various factories are likely to be dotted around areas of cheap, skilled labour, notably Asia. Those components in turn rely on minerals being extracted from all over the globe. The coating for a standard monitor alone contains compounds manufactured from sulfur, zinc, silver, bauxite, gold and a host of other minerals whose names are unfamiliar to all but mineralogists – alunite, azurite, boronite, enargite, cerargyrite, realgar and tetrahedrite – all mined or processed in countries that are often thousands of kilometres from where the computer will be assembled, let alone finally purchased and used.

To squeeze profits from such geographically dispersed sites of production, companies have increasingly adopted 'just-in-time' inventory systems, not least in order to cut down on the costs of traditional warehousing: trucks, trains and ships are effectively used instead as mobile warehouses. The slightest delay in transporting components can thus cause major financial losses. Similarly, the economies of scale that make mines such as Carajas in the Amazon commercially viable require 'huge deposits of high-quality ore to fill ships on a regular basis and with minimum delay in harbour' (Bunker and Ciccantell 2005, p. 2). In the calculus of global manufacturing chains, 'every day in ocean travel that a country is distant from the importer reduces the probability of sourcing manufactured goods from that country by 1 per cent' (World Bank 2009, p. 179).

Such pressures have not only resulted in the emergence of new physical geographies of production structured around special economic zones, transport hubs and infrastructure corridors; they are also spawning new forms of 'transportation governance' through computerised management programmes that allow logistics companies to match labour to demand in real time across multiple supply chains and even, using the 'big data' collected from consumers' web searches and other sources, to anticipate emerging consumer demand across countries and make appropriate changes to supply chains (Neilson and Rossiter 2014). Just as countries are now ranked for credit rating purposes by the extent to which they have introduced legislation enabling Public–Private Partnerships, so, too, they are now policed for their logistics infrastructure. Since 2007 the World Bank (2015b) has published an annual *Logistics Performance Index* (LPI) that measures how countries 'stack up' against each other in terms of their 'logistics "friendliness"' (homily from the bank (2012): 'a trade supply chain is only as strong as its weakest link'). In keeping with its role as the disciplinarian enforcer of neoliberalism, the bank ranks countries by the efficiency of their customs and border management, the quality of trade and transport infrastructure, the ability to track and trace consignments and the frequency with which shipments reach their intended destination on time. Industry consultants, such as McKinsey and Frost & Sullivan, similarly keep a close eye on the costs and speed of national transport systems, monitoring the dollar price of shipping a container load of goods to and from different countries ($400 to the United Kingdom from China, more than $1,000 from Nigeria); the number of documents that exporters have to fill in per shipment (eleven in Angola, six in South Africa); 'container dwell times' in different ports (global average, seven days; average in West Africa, eleven to thirty days), and so on (O'Carroll 2013; Rallaband 2013; Manyika 2014). Such tools are used to identify weak links in global supply chains. In response, China, Morocco, South Africa, Indonesia and Malaysia have all introduced specific government programmes to streamline and improve their logistics infrastructure.

5.2 Corridors, hubs and cities: a whistle-stop tour

The combined pressures of economies of scale, the off-shoring of manufacturing, the growth of a 'global consuming class' and just-in-time delivery systems are now playing out in 'a surge of infra-structural investments, enclosures and large-scale territorial planning strategies' (Brenner 2014) aimed at better integrating production, distribution and consumption on a global scale. No (inhabited) con-tinent is excluded: infrastructure masterplans have been drawn up (with little or no public consultation) for North, South and Central America, Africa, Asia, Europe, Australasia and the Arctic. The result is a potential (or actual) churning of geographies as efforts are made to restructure whole regions into 'hubs', 'transit zones', 'development corridors', 'export zones', 'spatial development initiatives', 'intercon-nectors' and 'intermodal logistics terminals', profoundly affecting the class focus of investment patterns.

For all the talk of providing poorer people with access to clean water or electricity, the planned (or already initiated) programmes are primarily directed at reducing 'economic distance', thereby unlocking remote mineral deposits and expanding the export of cheap agricultural produce; better harnessing landlocked countries to the global economy; expanding inland free trade zones and low-wage production centres that have to date been largely restricted to coastal areas; speeding supply chain connections; and improv-ing linkages between the 44 cities where the bulk of the 'global consuming class' are predicted to be living by 2025 (consultants McKinsey even chide investors that notions of 'emerging markets' are no longer 'helpful'; instead, business should think in terms of cities and the linkages between them (Dobbs *et al.* 2015)). Some of the plans are national in scale, others regional and still others continent-wide or (as in China's One Belt, One Road programme) near-global. But all have the goal of harnessing nature and the poor to the expansion of those forms of capital that profit from servicing, directly or indirectly, the one billion people whose incomes are high enough to make them significant consumers. And all would rely to a large extent for their finance on expanding the rents made available through Public–Private Partnerships.

Space does not allow a leisurely Grand Tour of the planned

projects, but a flying visit is possible. The proposals that have been drawn up for the cheap labour- and resource-rich continents of Africa, South America and Asia give an idea of the gargantuan scale of the planners' intentions. But before strapping in and buckling up, a quick word from the flight attendant: much as the planners might like to assume that it is their actions and intentions that will primarily determine the future of infrastructure, they are not the only characters who will write the story. Rocks, rivers, mountains, forests, machines, climate, weather, bacteria, furry and not-so-furry animals, legal texts, workers, peasants, indigenous peoples, slum dwellers, fishers, individual entrepreneurs, national parliaments and a myriad other human and non-human actors will also have a role: and it is the interplay among them that will ultimately determine whether or not the lines and blobs on the planners' map materialise or disappear, get moved, ignored or erased or are used for purposes that the planners never intended (Mitchell 2002). The future that the planners seek to colonise through their maps and plans is never assured. Many projects that exist on paper have already been abandoned or have ground to a halt: over the past four decades, for example, there have been five attempts to extend Bolivia's railway lines to Chile and Brazil, all of which have proved fruitless. While the plans signal the direction of travel that globalised forms of capital require if they are to expand, the ultimate trajectory is not written in the maps, masterplans and intergovernmental meetings about super-corridor futures, nor, indeed, inscribed within some presumed steam-roller logic behind global capitalism, whose coherence is never as coherent as theorists project. It will be determined by the ways in which those plans interact with other agents, human and non-human, both now and in the future. In that respect, the maps are as much maps of capital's vulnerabilities as they are of its claims on the future.

Africa

In Africa, where infrastructure inefficiencies are estimated to cost businesses $172 billion a year in lost growth (PIDA 2008), the blockages that poor transport creates for expansion of the mining, oil, gas and other natural resource industries are primarily shaping the geography of infrastructure investment. Africa has huge mineral resources – it is endowed with half of the world's known platinum, cobalt and diamond reserves, 40 per cent of the world's gold reserves and among the largest reserves of manganese and chromium – but without reliable transport routes that enable deposits to be extracted at scale, many mining operations cannot compete globally. Transporting a tonne of iron ore from Africa to China costs up to three times more than what it would cost from Australia. In many African countries, the capacity for transporting in bulk (thus achieving economies of scale) is simply not there. Mozambique, for instance, has rail capacity for transporting some six million tonnes of coal a year. China, by way of contrast, can transport a billion tonnes. As one industry pundit recently told *Transport World Africa*, 'Pulling the stuff out of the earth is not viable if it can't be moved' (Transport World Africa 2015). With mineral prices falling, it is a problem that is increasingly bedevilling mining schemes the world over: there are just too few ports and transport facilities capable of handling the vast quantities that need to be shipped to make mines viable (Nostromo Research 2015).

The 'spatial connections' that global capital now demands to further its expansion in Africa are continental in scope. To extract iron ore profitably from many of the new deposits that are being opened up in West and Central Africa, an estimated 4,000 km of new railway line will need to be laid (at an average cost of between $2 million and $5 million per kilometre) and new deep-water ports built along the coast. Guinea's giant Simandou iron ore concession, being developed by mining giant Rio Tinto, is illustrative of the scale of the required investment: to transport the extracted ore in sufficiently large quantities, a new 650-km railway is to be built through the mountains (requiring 35 bridges and 24 km of tunnels) to a new deep-sea port south of Conakry on the Morebaya river. The cost is estimated at $9 billion, some eight times Guinea's annual national budget, to be financed through a PPP.

Undaunted, the African Union's New Partnership for Africa's Development (NEPAD) has launched a 'spatial development initiative' (SDI) programme to unlock Africa's otherwise 'stranded' natural resources through better infrastructure connections. Modelled on the existing Maputo Development Corridor that links South Africa's landlocked industrial heartland in Gauteng province to a cargo port at Maputo in Mozambique (see Box 5.1 'The Maputo Development Corridor'), each SDI project is 'anchored' in a single resource-extraction project or a cluster of such projects whose cash flow and cargo volumes are supposedly high enough to underpin the financing of the railways, roads, pipelines, ports and other 'backbone' infrastructure necessary to make a corridor viable (SME-CSMI 2012). Once in place, this infrastructure is 'leveraged' to develop other industries whose cargo volumes would be too low to finance the corridor themselves. In Mozambique, for example, a satellite agriculture

Box 5.1 The Maputo Development Corridor

Transport corridors are not new to Africa. Many were developed during the colonial era to ship mineral resources from 'pit to port'. Few, however, were intended as platforms for generating wider economic development. The post-apartheid government of South Africa sought to change this through its 'spatial development initiatives' (SDI) programme, launched in 1995. The aim was to mobilise public and private finance for the targeted development of specific regions on the back of new or existing natural resource extraction projects.

One of the first SDIs to be developed was the Maputo Development Corridor, initiated in 1995. The corridor provides rail and road links from South Africa's landlocked industrial heartlands in the provinces of Gauteng and Mpumalanga to the port of Maputo in Mozambique. Gauteng is the largest gold-producing region in the world and home to South Africa's largest concentration of manufacturing industries, generating 40 per cent of South Africa's gross domestic product. Mpumalanga is a major coal- and platinum-producing area, containing 50 per cent of the country's known coal reserves and producing 76 per cent of its coal mining output. A spur from the main corridor connects Limpopo province to the main corridor. Limpopo is South Africa's third largest mining area, generating 9 per cent of the country's mining income.

Major industrial projects that have been developed in the corridor include BHP Billiton's Mozal aluminium smelter, the Pande/Temane gas field and associated gas pipeline, an iron pelletising plant, an iron and steel plant, a slurry pipeline, a magnetite dump upgrading plant, two coal-fired power stations and a major petrochemical plant.

The African Development Bank has described the Maputo Development Corridor as the 'most successful regional interconnection initiative in sub-Saharan Africa'. But many others view it as a top-down project, driven by a concern for logistics, which has side-lined smaller businesses in favour of megaprojects that have largely benefited multinationals. The World Bank has acknowledged that the 'trickle down effects have not been significant'.

Sources: Byiers and Vanheukelom 2014; Kunaka 2011; MCLI undated; NEPAD 2008; Porto de Maputo undated; Roodt 2007

development corridor is being canvassed as an offshoot to the existing Beira Corridor linking the port of Beira to Harare in Zimbabwe, which is being upgraded to reduce transport costs. The corridor would be anchored around the infrastructure being developed to exploit the open-cast metallurgical coal mine of the Brazilian mining multinational Vale at Moatize and that of the Australian company Riversdale at Banga. The plan is to develop 190,000 hectares of land for agro-industrial biofuel and sugar production, reportedly using smallholders as contract farmers (Beira Corridor undated; Kaarhus 2011; Paul and Steinbrecher 2013). The poor quality of existing rail links and port facilities, however, is said to be proving problematic for the two anchor projects (Transport World Africa 2015).

Over 30 development corridors have now been initiated in sub-Saharan Africa (see Exhibit 5.1). The majority are 'anchored' around mining projects but many have ancillary agricultural corridors or tourism developments as secondary offshoots. A race is on to develop the shortest corridor routes to the sea from Zambia's copperbelt province and the Democratic Republic of the Congo's mineral-rich Katanga province, with Angola, Tanzania, South Africa and Namibia all developing routes. Corridors serving iron ore, copper, coal, nickel and other mines are also planned in northern and central Mozambique, Botswana, Ghana, Liberia and Sierra Leone (Weng *et al.* 2013). In southern Africa, where 18 corridors have either already been constructed or are under construction, a 'seamless' road link ('seamless' is the adjective of the moment for transport planners) now exists between a port at Walvis Bay on Namibia's South Atlantic coast and Maputo on the Indian Ocean in Mozambique, reducing the time it takes to transport cargo from Europe to South Africa's commercial Gauteng province by five days. In eastern Africa, the upgraded 1,200-km Rift Valley rail line from Mombasa to Kampala has cut journey times for freight by half. Elsewhere, other ambitious transcontinental corridors are planned. A container mega-port is being developed at Lamu, off the Kenyan coast, to serve as the gateway for a multi-billion dollar export corridor, known as LAPSSET,[2] which would connect Kenya with South Sudan and Ethiopia via a new railway and road network. The LAPSSET corridor, which would include an oil pipeline and tourist resort developments, is itself part of an envisaged (but as yet largely unfunded) super-corridor plan – the Great Equatorial Land Bridge project – that would link Lamu on the Indian Ocean with Douala on the Atlantic.

Although many planned corridors have failed to attract anchor investors or have seen key investors withdraw – Rio Tinto, for example, recently sold its holdings in Mozambique's Riversdale coal mine, an anchor for the Beira Agricultural Development Corridor, after it was denied permits to ship coal by barge down the Zambezi River – the 'spatial development' plans keep coming. To ease transportation blockages between cities and open export routes, governments have

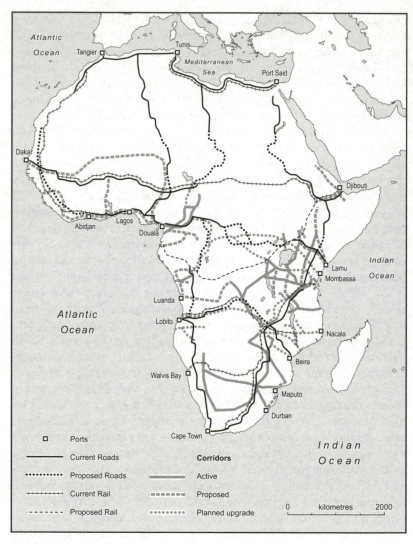

Exhibit 5.1 Development corridors in sub-Saharan Africa

agreed a continent-wide infrastructure 'masterplan', with the aim of 'placing Africa on an unstoppable growth trajectory as the continent gets more interconnected and integrated' (PIDA undated). As envisaged, 51 continental-scale energy, water and transport projects (some dusted down from previous, failed infrastructure plans) would be constructed by the year 2040, at a cost of $360 billion. A priority is the plugging of 'missing links' in the existing continental network of

Trans-African Highways, a project initiated forty years ago but as yet only three-quarters completed. To meet 'a meaningful level of connectivity', according to the World Bank, 60,000–100,000 km of new roads will need to be built (Foster 2008). Dozens of regional and national-level programmes are also on the drawing board, under construction or already completed, all aimed at expanding existing 'development' corridors or creating new ones. If completed, the planned infrastructure is expected to stimulate a six- to eight-fold increase in the volume of goods transported around Africa. Critically, transport times would be dramatically reduced. According to the UN Economic Commission for Africa, upgrading the road and rail links within the existing north–south corridor linking Dar es Salaam in Tanzania to Durban in South Africa through Zambia, Zimbabwe and Botswana would cut transport costs and transit times for traffic between Dar es Salaam and Lusaka by about one-quarter.

South America

No less ambitious plans are on the drawing board for South America. As in Africa, reducing the costs and time of transport (particularly for exports of minerals and agricultural produce) is uppermost in the planners' minds. Speeding the movement of goods is seen as paramount if South America is to compete globally. Brazil, for example, has a dismal ranking in the World Bank's 2014 index for the ease of trading across borders (116 out of 189) (World Bank 2014c), while the World Economic Forum judges its roads to be worse than those in Cote D'Ivoire, Ethiopia and Sierra Leone and its ports worse than those in Burundi and Burkina Faso (WEF 2014b). Only 14 per cent of the country's roads are paved, compared with half in China and India and more than 80 per cent in Russia, while the cost of exporting a container from Brazil is more than double the average in other member states in the OECD: typically, according to McKinsey Global Institute, it takes 5.5 days for inspected cargo to be released as against 2.2 days in the United States (Elstrodt *et al.* 2014). Brazil's railway network is also judged to be below par, with just 29,000 km of track, compared to 226,000 km in the United States, a country of similar size. Some ports also lack dedicated rail transport networks, using the same tracks as passenger trains, resulting in (and this is what really counts) delays. Up to 12 per cent of all grain produced in Brazil is reportedly lost to poor infrastructure, while congestion can mean that up to 89 ships are left queuing to dock on an average day at the port of Paranaguá (Romei 2013).

South America's response has been to adopt a continent-wide infrastructure masterplan, the 'Initiative for the Integration of Regional Infrastructure in South America' (IIRSA). Conceived by the Inter-American Development Bank and launched in 2000 by the 12 countries of what is now the Union of South American Nations (UNASUR), IIRSA aims to attain 'effective territorial connectivity' throughout the region by harnessing 'land, river, sea, and air ways' to the cause of trade facilitation (Communique of Brasilia 2000). The plan divides South America into ten 'Integration and Development Hubs' (in Spanish 'Ejes de Integración y Desarrollo' or EIDs),[3] each covering thousands of square kilometres (see Exhibit 5.2). The hubs are intended to 'concentrate current and potential trade flows'; 'support production chains and activities with economies of scale': expand export corridors; open up remote regions for resource extraction; improve 'just-in-time' logistics; capitalise on the fragmentation of global supply chains by encouraging manufacturers to relocate factories, service centres and head offices to the region; build regional markets; and put in place infrastructures that will serve 'the new affluent classes, the new middle classes, and the millions of inhabitants that will increase their consumption' (Barbero 2011, p. 34) primarily in South America and Asia. The masterplan is portrayed by planners as a 'make or break' project for South America. As Ariel Pares, a former IIRSA coordinator for Brazil, puts it, 'Without this kind of planned network of physical integration, South America would not stand a chance in the 21st century' (Friedman-Rudovsky 2012). Just *whose* chance and future in South America would be jeopardised is unstated.

IIRSA is now part of a wider strategic action plan developed by UNASUR's Committee of the South American Infrastructure and Planning Council (COSIPLAN) under which investments favouring US and Brazilian capital have increased. Under current proposals (IIRSA 2014a, 2014b, 2015), some 579 projects, costing an estimated $163 billion, have been identified, of which 89 per cent involve roads, airports, ports, inland waterways and 'multimodal' transport schemes, 9 per cent energy projects (almost exclusively, in the case of the Peru–Brazil–Bolivia hub and MERCOSUR–Chile hub, hydroelectric dams) and the rest communications infrastructure. Of these, 107 have been completed and 169 are under construction: the rest are still at the planning stage. Thirty-one projects are currently identified as 'priority' anchor initiatives, 91 per cent of them in the transport sector, the majority involving the transformation of over 8,000 km of rivers into industrial shipping channels.

Exhibit 5.2 IIRSA's ten 'Integration and Development Hubs'

The scale of the infrastructure now contemplated for IIRSA/ COSPLAN's ten Integration and Development Hubs is huge. Completion of the priority projects alone would see the construction of 7,000 km of new railway lines, two major tunnel systems (one 13 km long), six new sea ports, four river ports, six logistics centres, and the widening and deepening of several thousands of kilometres of waterways. In the Amazon hub, encompassing Brazil, Colombia, Ecuador and Peru, a prime focus is the linking of the Huallaga, Marañón, Morona, Ucayali and Putumayo rivers in the Amazon basin to the Pacific ports of Buenaventura in Colombia, Esmeraldas in Ecuador and Paita in Peru, creating export routes to Asia, Europe and the eastern United States that could compete on costs and time with the Panama Canal. Over three million cubic metres of sediment will need to be dredged from the rivers to make them navigable. In the Andean hub, two north–south road corridors are under construction to connect the main cities of Bolivia, Colombia, Ecuador, Peru and Venezuela, creating a market of about 103 million people 'with a GDP of $361,824.2 million' (IIRSA 2011). In addition, IIRSA aims to tap the 'great production potential' of the region's biodiversity for 'biotechnology, pharmaceutical and cosmetics', as well as boosting exports of oil, copper, gold and coal (IIRSA 2011). To the east, in the Guianese Shield hub (also known as the Amazon–Orinoco hub), a gas pipeline connecting Venezuela, Brazil and Argentina is planned, along with works to link the Amazon and Orinoco river basins so as to increase exports of uranium, iron and other minerals, and soybeans.

IIRSA (2011) insists that the hubs are more than 'mere corridors' between markets: their aim is nothing short of the restructuring of whole territories in order to cut 'the costs of moving in space', thereby reducing the costs of moving people and goods. Growth, trickle-down and the rest are presumed to follow, enabling South America to develop industries that will move the continent beyond a reliance on mining and agriculture. Politicians on the Left as much as the Right have embraced this strategy. For example, Ecuador's leftist president, Rafael Correa, has sought to use infrastructure corridors to catalyse a shift in the economy away from a dependency on exporting primary products and towards a 'bio-socialist' knowledge economy (Wilson *et al.* 2015a). But his plan to use an IIRSA transport corridor from the port of Manta to Manus in Brazil so as to spur the development of a 'bio-knowledge' university and a series of 'Millennium Cities' has failed to move Ecuador away from a reliance on mineral extraction: on the contrary, the corridor is being used to *increase* oil exploration, while the Millennium Cities have turned out to be less cities than 'towns of a few hundred inhabitants that resemble small-town America, with grids of individual white houses arranged around a school, a health centre, sports fields, a police station' (Wilson *et al.* 2015a, p. 15). Indeed, Correa's attempt to escape extractivism by embracing a reorganisation of the region through infrastructure programmes aimed at increasing its global competitiveness has, in the words of geographers Japhy Wilson, Manuel Bayón and Henar Diez, only ended up 'strengthening the powers that it is struggling to escape', at great cost to local communities whose prior connections to their territories have been violently disrupted.

Nonetheless, IIRSA's cheerleaders continue to portray the venture as a plan that will transform South America for 'all our South American people'. Opening the continent's first transoceanic highway in 2010, Alan García, then president of Peru, waxed lyrical about creating 'a road of social justice and well-being' (Friedman-Rudovsky 2012). Undoubtedly, the highway (like many other IIRSA projects) has cut transportation times and costs for business, particularly Brazilian agricultural and mineral exporters: in the year following the road's opening, for example, soy exports from Brazil to China rose by 7 per cent, bumping the US into second place as China's main soy provider. Contractors and investors from Europe and North America have also benefited hugely from the pipeline of projects (Vargas 2012), one-quarter of which are funded by the private sector alone or as Public–Private Partnerships. But for those whose livelihoods do not depend on bending to the World Bank or the World Economic Forum's global competitiveness indices, and whose sense of time, space, work, energy and 'infrastructure' is rooted in a different social and economic logic and rhythm, IIRSA's roads, waterways, railways and territorial disciplining have placed them at the sharp end of what David Harvey calls 'accumulation by dispossession' (Harvey 2004). It is a process they have long struggled against and continue to resist. Investors and their advisers may view IIRSA's hubs as embodying a new South America made up of 'vast tracts of land; liberalised, business-friendly regulatory regimes; major markets and a previously non-existent spending capacity' (Jaramillo 2015, p. 51). But they also embody the torn-to-shreds lives of smallholders whose land has been taken over for commercial production and of territories that have been mined, drilled, dredged and remodelled to realise IIRSA's 'spatial planning' ambitions. Unsurprisingly, IIRSA's projects, like other corridors elsewhere, have provoked fierce resistance, often violently suppressed, from local communities (see Box 5.2 'Corridors of violence'). For this, too, is one of the obstacles that capital must overcome if it is to annihilate the vast space of South America by time.

Box 5.2 Corridors of violence

Millions of people worldwide are potentially affected by the logistics corridors that planners have etched across world maps. Already conflicts have been sparked, as communities find their lands grabbed for industrial plantations or their livelihoods disrupted by roads, railways and other transport projects. In northern Mozambique, more than half a million people living in communities along the banks of the Lúrio river will be severely affected if plans are approved to realise the Lúrio River Valley Development Project (DVRL) in the controversial Nacala corridor. More than 100,000 people in the provinces of Niassa, Nampula and Cabo Delgado may lose their homes and land.

In many cases, conflicts over land, water, forests and commons have resulted in brutal repression. In Peru, protests erupted nationwide after police attacked over 3,000 indigenous people who had been blockading the Fernando Belaúnde Terry highway near the northern city of Bagua, which links the Amazon to the coast. Nine people were killed according to official figures. However, hospitals and religious organisations in the area reported a far higher death toll, possibly more than 40. Police are reported to have burned the bodies of slain protesters and dumped their remains in the river. Although protestors have been prosecuted, no legal action has been taken against the police officers involved or the politicians who are said to have given the green light for the shootings.

No less violent is the structural upheaval that the corridors bring in their wake, as peasant farmers are integrated (frequently against their wishes) into industrial plantations or disciplined into becoming workers in the mines or low-wage factories that the corridors serve. Huge numbers of displaced people are also recruited to build the megaprojects that the corridors rely on, in some cases working in conditions of near-slavery. Indeed, without the availability of a pool of cheap, displaced and marginalised labour to build the corridors, the 'time–space' annihilation demanded by capital would probably not be possible.

Once built, the corridors bring other forms of violence as newly opened up areas are reconfigured to meet the needs of commerce. Previous uses of land often become impossible – or are actively discouraged – while other new uses, such as mining or agribusiness, take hold, transforming whole territories in the process.

Sources: Arce 2009; Pambazuka News 2015;
LAWR 2009; Vargas 2015

Asia

By now, even this brief whistle-stop tour is running the risk of irksome repetition. Some passengers may be fidgeting in their seats. But the journey is almost over, and the most ambitious set of projects is yet to come.

Suffice it to say that all the countries of Asia have plans for major corridors to accelerate national and international transport links by 'devouring space to save time' (Nair 2015) or to increase 'connectivity' between major urban centres. The plans for Indonesia, the 'Greater Mekong subregion' (the Asian Development Bank's new geopolitical category for countries in the Mekong river basin) and India are emblematic:

- In Indonesia, six corridors are planned under an ambitious 15-year, $1 trillion Masterplan for Acceleration and Expansion of Indonesia's Economic Development, known as MP3EI, but likely to be renamed (although not substantially changed) as part of a review following major protests by social movements (AwasMIFEE 2015; Republic of Indonesia 2011; US Department of State 2013; Assegaf and Wiriasmoko 2013). Over 1,000 infrastructure and logistics projects are planned, including roads, railways (particularly to haul coal), airports and ports, with the goal of 'enhancing the flow of goods, services and information, reducing logistics costs and reducing cost inefficiencies' (Bappenas 2011). Each of the six interconnecting corridors is centred on developing key industries or natural resources (notably coal and palm oil) through clustered manufacturing hubs and Special Economic Zones (SEZs) (see Exhibit 5.3). The Java corridor, for example, has been allotted the task of being a 'Driver for National Industry and Service Provision'; the Kalimantan corridor that of being a 'Centre for Production and Processing of National Mining and Energy Reserves'; and the Sumatra corridor has been designated as a 'Centre for Production and Processing of Natural Resources and the Nation's Energy Reserves' (Bappenas 2011). Commenting on the impacts on the ground, which include major land grabs as companies seek to expand palm oil production, coal mining and other extractive industries, Indonesian activist Hendro Sangkoyo is blunt: 'It's a brutal class war out there' (Sangkoyo 2015a). Plans are also afoot for marine corridors to connect the islands of the Indonesian archipelago, a programme that is being promoted by the Association of Southeast Asian Nations (ASEAN) as part of a

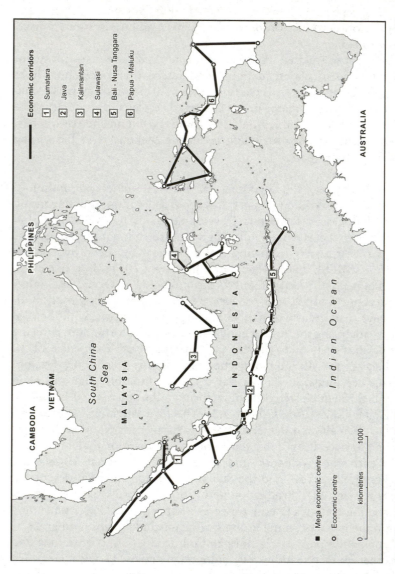

Exhibit 5.3 Indonesia's MP3EI economic corridors

wider 'nautical highway system' throughout Southeast Asia envisaged under its 'Master Plan on ASEAN Connectivity' (ASEAN 2010; Shekhar and Liow 2014). Militarisation of these proposed sea routes and the exclusion of local fisherfolk is anticipated.

- In the Greater Mekong subregion (consisting of Cambodia, China, Laos, Burma/Myanmar, Thailand and Viet Nam), at least 11 economic corridors are on the drawing board (see Exhibit 5.4). With the region now increasingly a site for cheap-labour manufacture of components, a key goal of planners is to enhance 'supply-chain connectivity' through more efficient logistics systems, stronger and deeper transport linkages, and cross-border trade facilitation. Here corridors are under active development. One corridor goes from east to west, running from Da Nang in Viet Nam through Laos and Thailand to Burma/Myanmar; the second from north to south, linking Kunming in China, Laos and Burma/Myanmar to Bangkok in Thailand, with a spur running from Nanning in China to Ha Noi and Hai Phong in Viet Nam; and the third connecting the southern part of Thailand, Cambodia and Viet Nam (Brunner 2013; ADB/ADBI 2009). Four of the countries – Cambodia, Laos, Thailand and Viet Nam – have also established an informal forum, the Mekong River Commission (MRC), to develop the Mekong river basin, including the re-engineering of the river between Simao (Cambodia) and Luang Prabang (Laos) to make it navigable for commercial shipping.
- In India, a vast infrastructure programme is underway to cut what consultants McKinsey call India's 'waste in logistics' (McKinsey & Company undated) and allow it to 'catch up' with China. Seven dedicated freight train corridors are planned or under construction; multiple projects are being implemented to increase the capacity of the country's 12 major ports whose throughput of iron ore, coal and containers is expected to increase by 146 per cent, 225 per cent and 818 per cent respectively over the next decade (IPA 2007); and five industrial development corridors (each with 'nodal' Smart Cities and core industrial hubs) are being developed, including the Amritsar–Kolkata Industrial Corridor, the Bengaluru–Mumbai Economic Corridor, the Chennai–Bengaluru Industrial Corridor and the Delhi–Mumbai Industrial Corridor (see Exhibit 5.5) (Consulate General of India 2014). Of these corridors, the Delhi–Mumbai Industrial Corridor (DMIC) is billed as the largest single infrastructure project in the world. Stretching over thousands of square kilometres, it would consist of a high-speed railway line, exclusively for freight, to India's largest

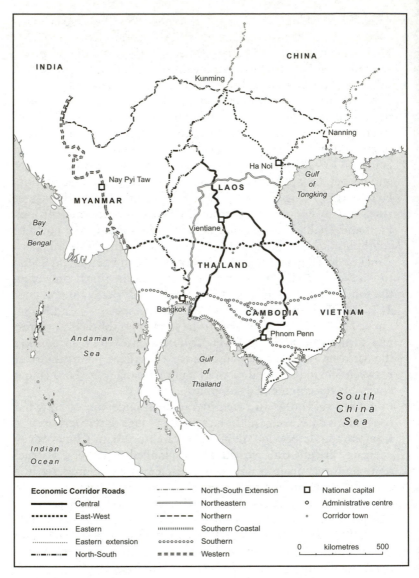

Exhibit 5.4 Transport corridors in the 'Greater Mekong subregion'

container port, near Mumbai; 23 manufacturing centres; six airports; two power plants; a six-lane highway; and 24 new Smart Cities, each planned to house three million people (Kumar 2015). The objective is to expand India's manufacturing and services

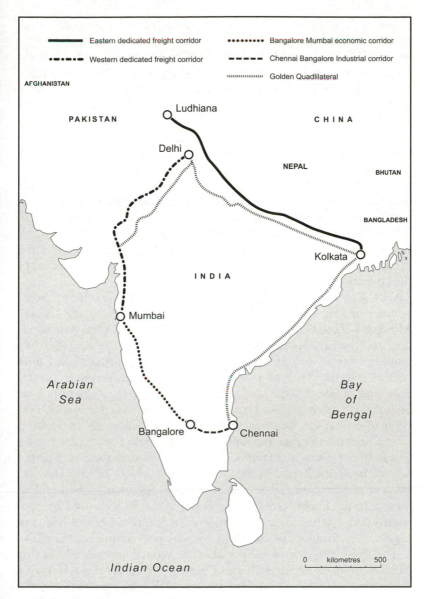

Exhibit 5.5 India's economic corridors

base and develop DMIC as a 'Global Manufacturing and Trading Hub' (DMICDC 2015). Approximately 180 million people will be affected, many of whom are likely to be displaced, creating the potential for major conflict (Guttal 2014).

But the Big Daddy of attempted time–space annihilation (and, some would argue, of contemporary struggles for regional hegemony) is China's 'One Belt, One Road' (OBOR) programme, officially launched in 2013. Encompassing 60 countries (thus potentially half of the world), OBOR is intended to create a network of free trade areas connected by both terrestrial and marine corridors stretching from the Pacific to the Baltic Sea (see Exhibit 5.6 and Box 5.3 'Made in the World @ World Trade Organization') (NRDC-PRC 2015). The aim, according to Li Chunhong, a deputy to the National Peoples' Congress and head of the Guangdong Provincial Development and Reform Commission, is 'to strengthen infrastructure connectivity with our neighbours, simplify customs clearance procedures and build international logistics' (Xinhua 2015). According to the Shaanxi Administration of Surveying, Mapping and Geoinformation, a detailed survey has already been completed of the 'geographic, transportation, culture and economic' characteristics of the countries along the route (Xinhua 2015).

OBOR's 'belt' (officially the 'New Silk Road Economic Belt') consists of four land corridors: the Eurasia land bridge; the China–Mongolia–Russia corridor; the China–Central Asia–West Asia corridor; and the China–Indochina Peninsula corridor. Collectively, they would connect China, Central Asia, Russia and Europe; link China with the Persian Gulf and the Mediterranean Sea through Central Asia and Western Asia; and connect China with Southeast Asia, South Asia and the Indian Ocean. The 'road' is in fact a marine corridor (the '21st-Century Maritime Silk Road') designed 'to go from China's coast to Europe through the South China Sea and the Indian Ocean in one route, and from China's coast through the South China Sea to the South Pacific in the other' (NRDC-PRC 2015). The corridor would involve not only shipping but, reportedly, deep seabed mining in the Indian Ocean. The Belt and the Road would be connected via a 3,000 km transportation corridor from China's Xinjiang region to Pakistan's Chinese-built Gwadar port on the Arabian Sea.

The land corridor would massively reduce journey times for exports from China to Europe. Currently, Chinese manufacturers transport their products to the coast and then halfway around the world by sea: the journey takes up to 60 days – 'an eternity for the latest iPads and other "fast fashion" products' (*The Economist* 2014b). By contrast, transporting goods overland by train takes 14 days. The existing rail connections run infrequently – the German logistics group DB Schenker recently began a weekly train shipment from the coastal city of Chongqing, where Hewlett Packard and

Box 5.3 Made in the World @ World Trade Organization

Annihilating space by time is about more than just bigger and faster railways and roads or deeper and larger ports and airports. The corridors now being planned (and constructed) are also conceived as free trade zones, where tariffs are progressively removed – and with them the border controls, paperwork and other 'man-made barriers' that, in the words of the World Bank, 'increase distance' by slowing down the transport of goods.

As such, argues Indonesian activist Hendro Sangkoyo, the corridors may be seen as building blocks for what the World Trade Organization terms a 'Made in the World' economy, in which supply chains, not nations, organise global economic geography. It is a world in which 'exports' would disappear (no product being a product of any one country); in which 'outsourcing' has no meaning for companies since, in terms of production, 'there is no "out" and no "in" any more'; and where 'what counts for success' for nations 'is not so much the production and sale of final goods but using national comparative advantages to add most value along the production chain'.

To achieve 'integrated corridor management', the planners are not simply thinking in terms of free trade agreements that would remove tariff barriers between countries. They also envisage specific legal regimes that would apply just to the corridors, especially where they are shared by a number of countries, in order to ensure 'freedom of transit for cargo' (a formulation that effectively claims rights for cargo) and uniform environmental and other legislation. These new legal regimes do not feature on the planners' maps, but are central to the planners' vision.

One touted model for future corridors is the legal regime that was negotiated (in secret) for oil multinational BP's Baku–Tbilisi–Ceyhan oil pipeline corridor, stretching from the Caspian through Azerbaijan, Georgia and Turkey to the Mediterranean. Under the legal agreements for the project, the BP-led pipeline consortium is exempt from any obligations under Azerbaijani, Georgian and Turkish law, other than the constitutions of the three countries. Where any national law conflicts with the pipeline agreements, the agreements win out. Exemptions have already been successfully claimed against environmental laws. Moreover, should any of the countries introduce legislation that affects the 'economic equilibrium' (read current and future profits) of the project, they are obliged to compensate the consortium.

This is the world of corridors, spatial development initiatives and 'Made in the World'.

Sources: Friedman 2012; Green 2013; Government of Turkey 1999; Hildyard and Muttitt 2006; VCCSII 2011; WTO 2011, 2015

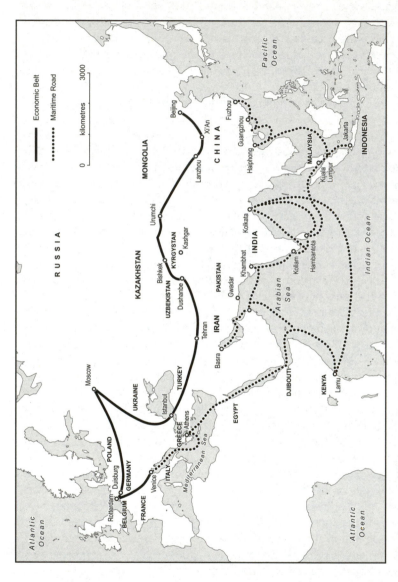

Exhibit 5.6 One Belt, One Road

Apple supplier Foxconn have factories, to Duisburg in Germany via Kazakhstan, Russia, Belarus and Poland – and the poor quality of the transport links in Central Asia adds considerably to the time. To break what Xi Jinping, China's president, calls the 'connectivity bottleneck', tracks are being improved and a new inland terminal (known as a 'dry port') and rail yard are being built in Kazakhstan. Sinotrans, China's state-owned logistics company, aims to add 12 new lines that would provide a 'door-to-door' service to destinations in Europe, including Leipzig, Nuremberg, Stuttgart, Munich, Brussels, Vienna, Budapest, Prague and Amsterdam, in the near future (Zhang Zhao 2015). The frequency of trains would also be increased to one a day. Although the overland rail route is currently twice as expensive as transporting by sea, the gap is narrowing as manufacturers in Europe start filling what have often been empty carriages going back to China 'with high-priced products such as luxury cars' (*The Economist* 2014b).

Domestically, the New Silk Road is intended to encourage the expansion of Chinese manufacturing away from the coast to western China or abroad. Within China, the project is already well under way, with several provinces building logistics centres, aviation, rail and highway networks, bonded warehouses, new cities and IT centres. Other provinces have chosen to back elements of the plan that are outside China: the coastal powerhouse of Guangdong is reported to be supporting a power plant in Vietnam, banana plantations in Southeast Asia and a 5-million-tonne oil refining project in Burma/Myanmar (EIU 2015; Xinhua 2015). Indeed, a major plank of the OBOR project would appear to be to expand supply chains and networks *outside of* China while simultaneously ensuring that they remain centred *on* China (Kaminska 2015).

5.3 Frontier finance: whose cupboard is bare?

Huge sums of money would be required to implement all of these continent-wide masterplans aimed at resolving global capital's time–space dilemma and easing its future expansion. If implemented in full, the infrastructure planned for Asia would cost an estimated $8 trillion (Stokes 2015). China has said that it will stump up over $1 trillion for OBOR alone. Various sources are being mobilised, including a specially created $40 billion Silk Road Fund; a new subsidiary of CIC, China's Sovereign Wealth Fund, called CIC Capital, with a target of $100 billion; recapitalisations of the China Development Bank and China Exim Bank, each with close to $50 billion; and the

Maritime Silk Road Bank. But even China's pockets are not deep enough to go it alone. Two new Chinese-driven multilateral development banks, the Asian Infrastructure Investment Bank (with an initial capital base of $100 billion, of which $40 billion comes from China) and the New Development Bank (or 'BRICS bank') are also being enlisted for support. Even so, there is still a major funding shortfall.

The same is true for corridor plans elsewhere. Many of the individual projects, and certainly the wider schemes as a totality, are simply beyond the resources that can be raised through historical forms of infrastructure finance. Take the mining projects that are intended to act as anchor investments for many of the corridors in Africa. In the past, mining companies have generally funded the dedicated infrastructure that connects 'pit to port' off their own balance sheets, albeit often with guarantees from multilateral development banks and tax breaks and other subsidies from states. But this is no longer an option for most new mines. The routes are too long and the scale of the infrastructure too costly, particularly for small- to medium-sized mines, for a single operator to finance by themselves. A study by the World Bank's International Finance Corporation found just one greenfield mining project that was 'bankable' as a purely privately financed project (di Borgo 2012). Even if mining companies were to join together to share the infrastructure costs (as the IFC and others are keen to encourage them to do, but which the companies resist for reasons of competition), only half would be viable. Nor are African governments in a position to finance the projects on their own: as the IFC notes, most 'do not appear to possess the sovereign borrowing capacity, or the budgetary capability, to provide meaningful financing for large-scale mining-related infrastructure projects' (IFC 2013, p. 44). The costs are also beyond the wherewithal of private banks, even when acting in concert, not least because of the need to repair bank balance sheets and rebuild capital and liquidity buffers following the 2008 global financial crisis. Although some projects could be financed by bringing in multilateral sources of finance, such as the World Bank, such sources could not conceivably finance all the projects that capital needs for its 'annihilate space by time' demands.

Globally, there is a massive gap between the available funding for new infrastructure and the amounts said to be needed between now and 2020 to 'meet the infrastructure demand from industry and households' (World Bank *et al.* 2015, p. 6). Some estimate that $50–70 trillion will need to be raised between now and 2030, of which about 37 per cent would be for infrastructure in emerging countries. This would mean finding $0.5 trillion to $1.5 trillion every year over and above what is currently being spent – and that is just for road, rail, port, airport, water and telecom development: schools, hospitals and other social infrastructure would be extra. The shortfall in the transport sector alone is an estimated $260 billion every year between now and 2030. The shortfalls in the energy sector are even higher – some $530 billion a year (OECD 2015c). A study for the 2015 meeting of the leaders of the G20 was blunt: 'Traditional funding sources will not be sufficient to meet these financing gaps' (World Bank *et al.* 2015, p. 6).

But let's be clear about one thing: there *is* more than enough public funding available to ensure heating, lighting, healthcare, clean water and other amenities for ordinary people, the more so were governments to replenish their depleted coffers by abandoning the low-tax regimes imposed through neoliberal structural adjustment programmes, or by clamping down on tax evasion and capital flight. The 'deficit' lies elsewhere: in the finance for the infrastructure that capital needs to expand. And, as in the past, capital has few options but to attempt to expand the pool of finance on which it can draw. The joint stock company, for example, arose in part to raise the huge sums needed to finance the infrastructure capital needed in the 1860s (as Marx remarked, without joint stock, 'the world would still be without railways' (Marx 2010, n.p.) – it would simply have taken too long for any owner-capitalist acting alone to accumulate capital sufficient for their construction (Hildyard and Lohmann 2014)). Likewise, multilateral development banks and syndicated bank loans emerged to finance post-colonial infrastructure development in the global South. Today, capital must similarly move to tap new sources of finance, in this instance wider capital markets, if it is not to implode. Hence the development of infrastructure-as-asset-class. And hence the push for Public–Private Partnerships (which are central to every one of the proposed corridors) to provide both an enticement to private investors and the foundation stone on which other extractive forms of finance can be built.

It is an agenda that is far from complete and far from a *fait accompli*. On the contrary, it has vulnerabilities that no amount of cynical casting of the problem in terms of 'keeping the lights on' or 'providing clean water for the poor' can disguise. For this is an agenda that explicitly abandons any pretence of achieving 'spatially balanced' development ('some [areas] must get rich before others' (World Bank 2009, p. 73)); that needs to treat people as mere pawns to be moved at the whim of planners (to repeat: 'No country has grown to riches without changing the geographic distribution of its people'

(World Bank 2009, p. 27)); and that pits the interests of globalised business against those whose livelihoods are organised not around just-in-time delivery systems but around the collective right of all to survive. To describe it as 'class war' is not to indulge in sloganising agitprop: it is to be candid about both its intent and its articulation. Make no mistake: when the wealth of one group in society rests on deliberately trashing the livelihoods of another, class conflict is unavoidable and inevitable. And, as discussed in the next chapter, it is in such emerging class conflicts that the most fertile ground for shifting the direction of travel is likely to emerge.

Notes

1 Defined as 'individuals with disposable incomes of more than $10 a day' (Dobbs *et al.* 2012).
2 LAPSSET – Lamu Port South Sudan Ethiopia project.
3 Initially twelve hubs were proposed, then nine. Currently, there are ten being developed (IIRSA 2011).

Chapter 6
Reflections for activism

> The power of capital lies not so much in its repressive apparatus (immense though it is), but rather in its ability to terrorise us with our lack of capacity to organise the reproduction of our lives outside of its structures.
>
> (Caffentzis 2009, p. 26)

> The future of humanity depends now on our being able to bring to life within the old, rotten and increasingly violent capitalism, flashes, intimations, anticipations, fragments of the world of dignity that we want to create.
>
> (Holloway 2009, p. xvii)

And so to the final chapter of this book – but not, one hastens to add, of infrastructure-as-asset-class, let alone of accumulation or of injustice. Those 'final chapters' will never be final: they will always be works-in-progress, unfolding, multi-layered narratives whose trajectory will be driven, as in the past, by the evolving interplay of numerous everyday struggles between those who would use mundane acts of provisioning (whether of food or water or healthcare or transport or goods or finance) as a means of accumulating wealth and those who would harness them to support social relationships and activities founded on the survival-oriented responsibility of all for each other's welfare. Activists on all sides duck and weave their way around obstacles, making use of what is at hand in attempts (some more successful than others) to construct the social and political relationships that might block or otherwise unsettle the other side's moves and assist in 'creating the world that they want'. Compromises abound (they are unavoidable), yet never entirely settle the inextricably interwoven and constantly erupting conflicts between provisioning-as-exploitation and provisioning-as-commoning. Every such compromise merely lays the ground for the next conflict, as social, economic and political forces at every level are constituted and reconstituted. There is no end of history.

This may seem obvious but needs stating, if only by way of a corrective to the delusion that a credible, transformative response to the question 'What is to be done?' can emerge from forms of organising that ignore this dynamic or treat it as a distraction, either from impatience or on the mistaken assumption that PPPs, infrastructure corridors, private equity funds, credit enhancement schemes and stabilisation clauses can be understood, let alone challenged, other than as political processes. Leaving aside the many further questions prompted by the question 'What is to be done?' (about what? by whom? on whose say-so? in what context? why are you asking? and so on), a 'to do' list that treats infrastructure-as-asset-class simply as a collection of innovative financial instruments to be analysed and acted upon in the abstract, without regard to their history, the role that infrastructure now plays in accumulation or the many and varied conflicts that this has engendered, is a 'to do list' that misses most of what is novel and important about infrastructure-as-asset-class. Unmindful (perhaps even ignorant) of the politics of these underlying conflicts, it is also a 'to do' list that is unlikely to engage with the constantly evolving strategic and tactical concerns of those struggles that constitute the most promising vectors for shifting the trajectory of finance's 'infrastructure' (even though, counter-intuitively for some activists, these may well be struggles that have no overt connection to either 'infrastructure' or 'finance'). And, as such, it is a 'to do' list that has an explosive potential to undermine, not strengthen, the building of effective alliances for change – and to place activists on the wrong side in a cluster of increasingly bitter struggles (Hildyard and Lohmann 2014).

This is important: because whatever issue one chooses, it is the relative organising power of different social movements, *including* capital, that determines the outcomes of the struggles among them and, hence, their direction of travel. Indeed, those struggles are as much struggles over organising itself, over strategy and tactics, as they are about specific grievances. A 'what is to be done?' response that fails to explore, be baffled by or approach with humility the complexities of organising as a social and political process is thus unlikely to evolve realistic strategies capable of shifting the trajectories of accumulation, injustice or 'infrastructure', or to be sensitive to changing dynamics that render existing strategies inadequate to new political circumstances.

But activists hoping for some 'blueprint' or 'rule book' for organising or for a 'masterplan' complete with ready-to-implement policies that take account of the wider trajectories of 'infrastructure-as-asset-class' or accumulation, will be disappointed. No such blueprint, rule book or masterplan exists, nor can they ever exist, precisely because activism must always cope with the antagonisms, tensions and contradictions within capital that drive history. The 'what is to be done?' question is thus constantly changing as it responds to and confronts new circumstances, new conflicts, new interests, new alliances, new contradictions and new power structures. There is no 'road map' for getting from 'here' to 'there' because 'here' and 'there' are processes, not places; neither 'capital' nor 'commons' can be pinpointed in time and place any more than 'living' or 'loving' can be, because they are verbs, not nouns (Linebaugh 2008; Caffentzis 2009, 2012). No strategy map can conceivably include every contour of the terrain on which activism operates because that terrain is constantly shifting as activists respond to new opportunities and blockages. No ready-made class or sets of alliances exist that can be 'mobilised' to 'implement' a preconceived 'masterplan' because there is no class that is not constantly being formed and reformed, no alliance that is not contingent on social, political and economic relationships that are shaped and reshaped in response to other alliances. And there is no all-encompassing set of global policies that could conceivably assist every struggle because all struggles are dialectical.

Instead there are questions that might assist activists on their journey. How might they better understand the dynamics of the destructive trajectories in which they seek to intervene? How might they enlist the support of others in developing such an understanding? How might their activism better inform constructive and collective interventions in the struggles that define the dynamics of infrastructure-as-asset-class and accumulation? What approaches to activism might they build on? What approaches might it be wiser to avoid? What blockages might a more effective activism need to understand and confront? To what struggles might it look for exploring ways forward?

These are not simple questions – and none of them have answers that do not themselves prompt more questions, to which the answers simply give rise to still further questions. Activists seeking to understand infrastructure-as-asset-class can build on a range of existing refusals by social movements to give consent to PPPs, privatisation, land grabs, pension grabs, forced evictions, free trade agreements, corporate subsidies, the squeezing of labour and other assaults on the commons; but efforts to challenge the trajectory of infrastructure-as-asset-class (and to exploit the vulnerabilities that it exposes for capital) are likely to be more effective if critical attention is paid to the many questions that surround contemporary ways of organising for change. For that reason, this chapter seeks to encourage a conversation beyond the specifics of particular campaigning opportunities. How might activism around infrastructure-as-asset-class strengthen itself by taking account of the wider movements of capital, and by allying itself more closely with commons-oriented movements to build or buttress social institutions that recognise the collective right of all (rather than the few) to survival?

6.1 The cry of injustice

A starting point, at least in respect of 'infrastructure-as-asset-class', might be to recognise that the vast majority of people are unlikely ever to experience its day-to-day impacts as a financial abstraction. They will (and do) encounter it as hikes in their water bills or their electricity being cut off because they can no longer afford to pay the bills; as engineers turning up uninvited to survey their land; as bulldozers tearing up forest commons on which they and their fellow villagers rely for fodder, timber or gatherable foods; as legal notices informing them that their land has been expropriated; as concrete being poured into rivers to dam or divert the flows of water where they fish, swim and play; as long hours, paltry pay and overwork in free trade zone factories; as the dismantling of long-fought-for public healthcare and educational services; and as the rich getting richer while the poor get poorer. In a word: as 'injustice'.

Different people (not just those directly affected) will react differently to such injustice. For many sympathetic activists in non-governmental organisations (NGOs), the response is generally mediated by bureaucratic imperatives, whatever their own personal views. Can the injustice be fitted into a pre-existing programme for which the NGO has funding to work? Does it fit with the human rights/development/environment/anti-corruption remit of the organisation? If it does, the injustice can then be probed for angles that assist that work. Nothing wrong with that: those at the sharp end of a land grab or a dam may well welcome the solidarity links that this potentially encourages. But there is a danger that, in the process, injustice is transformed into something that it is not, cutting off avenues for activism that may be more effective in challenging its trajectory.

An NGO seeking to fit 'infrastructure-as-asset-class' into a campaign to reform the World Bank, for example, may be constrained for institutional reasons from viewing it other than as a series of infrastructure projects in which the World Bank has an involvement. Reaching for the policy stethoscope, its diagnosis of the injustices that arise from these projects is likely to be channelled, wittingly or unwittingly, towards failures of World Bank lending practices. Were the World Bank's environmental and social safeguard policies applied? If they were, then the dose may not have been strong enough or the patient may need extra supervision to ensure that the medicine is properly applied. If they weren't, then new procedures clearly need to be introduced to ensure that they are in future. When a perusal of the patient's medical notes reveals that the bank's support for the projects is via a private equity fund, rather than directly from the bank, and that such intermediated finance is not subject to direct World Bank supervision, the prescription may seem clear: extend the safeguard policies to intermediated funding. A quick rummage through the policy medicine chest may also result in extra measures to address specific failings of the bank's existing policies: a course of 'enhanced participatory consultation' or the regular application of a soothing gender balm, suitably fortified with the latest formulation of 'prior informed consent' or 'labour standards'. Maybe, in extreme cases, a shot of land reform. Meanwhile, more alternative practitioners (perhaps including this author) hover at the door, urging a course of action that has been properly formulated with added 'class analysis'.

Of course this is a caricature; and apologies are due for any perceived violence it does to the dedicated work of numerous NGO workers around the world. But the view of 'injustice' as a patient that has succumbed to a malady that can be remedied through policy change deserves to be questioned. The problem does not lie in campaigning to hold the World Bank and other development finance institutions to account for failing to do what they say they will do: of course this needs to be done. Equally, the problem is not within attempts to make World Bank lending conditional on safeguard policies: of course these are needed, even though they are inadequate as tools for challenging the looting that infrastructure-as-asset-class enables or the World Bank's push to widen pools of finance to fund the infrastructure that capital wants. But care must be taken not to transform justice (and injustice) into something that, although amenable to policy campaigning, does not reflect what injustice actually is. A dam project or a land grab does not become 'just' because the right policy boxes have been ticked. For justice, like class, is an evolving set of relationships that are never fixed but are constantly being created and recreated. For this and other reasons, social justice cannot be achieved by inserting it as a policy into a project: it does not exist in a form that can ever be 'inserted'.

Viewed as a policy failure, injustice becomes largely a matter of persuading 'policy makers' in powerful institutions (the World Bank, the G8, the G20, national governments, corporations and the like) to do the right thing. But for many activists, particularly those who are not constrained by the bureaucracy of funded campaigns, institutional remits or departmental boundaries, the response to injustice does not start with policy prescriptions because injustice is not seen only as a policy issue. Instead, as Larry Lohmann of The Corner House reflects, based on over thirty years' experience of working with grassroots social movements:

> When the cry of injustice goes up from a crowd, it is usually an expression of a consciousness in the making. What's happening to us? How does it happen? How does it work? Who is doing this to us? How are they making alliances against us? What alliances should we make?
>   This is a dynamic process of discussion and enlightenment. And it involves what Ashish Nandy, the Indian political psychologist, used to call an expansion in the awareness of oppression.
>
> (Lohmann 2015b)

This is a very different approach to justice-as-bullet-points or justice as 'a ready-made thing' that can be 'put into any existing project, no matter how unjust'. It is more 'a discovery of oppression and discovery of strategies for dealing with it'.

The differences in approach are many but a number are worth exploring in more depth, since they are particularly relevant to evolving credible political responses to the question 'what is to be done?' For starters, the 'policy demands' that emerge (as they invariably do) from justice-as-discovery are not demands that are shaped by an abstract notion of 'justice' or by what might best resonate with a busy parliamentarian or some imaginary group of supremely powerful global or national regulators. They arise from the pressing need to build alliances and to expand political space. They are born not of 'politics as the art of the possible' but, in the words of Slovenian philosopher Slavoj Žižek, of politics as 'the art of the impossible' (Žižek 1999, p. 199). This does not preclude making policy demands that are directed at reforming existing institutions; but the interventions needed are those that are intended to change, not take for granted, 'the very parameters of what is considered "possible" in the existing constellation' (Žižek 1999, p. 199). Consequently their audience is primarily other social movements, allies within academia, sympathetic government officials and others with whom alliances – some tactical, some longer-term and more rooted – are sought that that will unsettle, bypass, undermine and change 'the very framework that determines how things work' (Žižek 1999, p. 199). Approaches that lock activism into engaging exclusively with specific reforms delivered by specific institutional targets (the World Bank, the G20, the latest UN conference) are likely to prove too parochial to offer such strategic alliance-building opportunities. Indeed, for the most part, such activism is predicated on permanently setting aside 'the art of the impossible' just to ensure a seat at the table. Efforts to make incremental improvements to safeguard policies cannot by themselves address the reality of infrastructure finance as looting. On the contrary, they rely, as one NGO worker of my acquaintance has frankly confessed, on 'educating' those who might wish to raise the issue into remaining silent about it.

A further difference between justice-as-ready-made-thing and justice-as-discovery is that social justice is not only a process of policy development. The 'process of discovery' is not some treasure hunt in which the jewel of 'justice' is uncovered, resplendently cut by some past jeweller. The process of discovery *itself* shapes 'justice' through the relationships it forms and the new class conflicts that may emerge from those relationships. Who one travels with in this process is critical and the connections between struggles that are made, ruptured and reworked in the process are what allow those struggles to breathe and to expand. What makes for robust alliances is not just convergence on 'policy'. This would be to misconstrue the process of 'consciousness in the making' that lies at the core of justice-as-discovery. For this is a consciousness that is sparked by something much more visceral and significant than an academic comparison of 'policy positions'. It is a product of those flashes of mutual recognition where people come to see something of their own struggle in someone else's, and vice versa; where they come to identify with others who may have quite *different* interests and to whom they may previously have been indifferent or even opposed; and where they are drawn together not so much because they come from or are 'embedded in absolute sameness', but because they come to realise that their life courses are being 'determined by ultimately similar processes and outcomes' (Palmer 2014, p. 49). In this process, they open themselves up to the realisation of something previously unrecognised, shifting the boundaries of what is 'possible' in the process.

It is through such processes that classes are formed. For class is not a ready-made category into which people are slotted because they share some set of definable interests: workers do not become working class because they work in a factory (Sewell 1986), any more than those who sign up to a pension scheme become capitalists. As the historian E.P. Thompson (1991, p. 10) has so powerfully argued, class is defined by people 'as they live their own history, and, in the end, this is its only definition'. Viewed synchronically, 'there are no classes but simply a multitude of individuals with a multitude of experiences' (Thompson 1991, p. 10). But viewed diachronically, patterns emerge as people respond to those experiences – of suffering, of loss, of aspirations and hopes, of fallings out and comings together, as well as of dispossession, low pay, union organising, strikes and lockouts – in ways that shape 'their relationships, their ideas and their institutions' (Thompson 1991, p. 10). It is through this reshaping of relationships that articulated identities emerge, fade and re-emerge in new forms as different groups in society come to appreciate what they have in common – and how that new shared sense of 'We' sets them apart from (and is usually opposed to) the interests of particular other 'We's' in society. And it is this shared 'We' that make class.

Again, this is not a singular process but one that involves multiple tensions, temporary resolutions and further tensions, not least because of the ambivalent positions that most people have in relation to both capital and the commons at different times in their lives. A worker whose job depends on just-in-time delivery systems may be fearful of opposing infrastructure that benefits the company she works for, but simultaneously be a victim of the company's labour-squeezing disciplines or of the free-trade policies that infrastructure corridors build. Class is not built simply by pointing out to her where she stands theoretically in relation to capital. It is built, as geographer David Harvey argues, by recognising the ambivalence of her position (and that of others), by discussing and understanding the ambivalences, by exploring their tensions and causes, and by asking 'if and how we want to put checks on the processes of capital accumulation' (Harvey 2008, n.p.).

6.2 Friendship as 'the political tool of the moment'

A social justice that is rooted in and shaped by such processes of discovery demands a practice and approach to politics that is very different from the approach adopted, either through inclination or bureaucratic imperative, by many professionalised non-governmental organisations. This is not an activism that rejects reports or demonstrations or lobbying; but it is an activism that emphasises mutual learning and unlearning, an understanding of each other's histories and political context, the building of relationships of care and trust, and respectful dialogue; and it places these processes over and above short-term, in-and-out, often opportunistic priorities of 'campaigns' that are often driven by funding or the need to present 'policy' to the next international conference. Above all, it is activism that emphasises patience, listening, solidarity and comradeship as the basis for collective action in defence of commons; and, beyond that, as seedbeds for cultivating the 'disciplined, self-denying, careful, tasteful friendships' that renegade priest and social activist Ivan Illich (1996, n.p.) identified as the 'supreme flowering of politics' and the very basis of community. As Illich remarks, 'a society will only be as good as the political result of [its] friendships'; those founded on mutuality and a shared commitment to collective survival – on commoning – will produce a very different society from those based on competition, accumulation and 'capital-ing' (Lohmann 2015c), one that is better equipped to resist the temptations of capital and its enclosing web of depredations (Esteva 2014).

This is an activism that would recognise (and not be flummoxed by) Mexican activist Gustavo Esteva's contention that 'friendship' is the 'political tool of the moment' (Esteva 2013). Indeed, for many activists, the enclosure of the commons is experienced first as a fracturing of friendships, and only later as politics: and it is partly this experience that brings forth the cry of injustice. The enclosures that make an infrastructure corridor possible cannot be reduced to land lost for a road or forests fenced off for an environmental offset project or the evictions that result from the construction of a new factory; nor can they be compensated for through cash. Enclosure tears apart friendships, both human and non-human, changing the ways in which people relate to their land, rivers and forests, their labour and their means of livelihood. It reorganises society to try to meet the overriding demands of the market. It demands that production and exchange conform to rules that reflect the exigencies of supply and demand, of competition and maximisation of output, of accumulation and economic efficiency. It inaugurates what Illich has called 'a new ecological order', changing relationships of power between people and groups of people by undermining or eroding many of the commoning friendships that ensured that survival was 'the supreme rule of common behaviour, not the isolated right of the individual' (Illich 1983, n.p.). It scoffs at the notion that there can be 'specific forms of community respect' for parts of the environment that are 'neither the home nor wilderness', but lie 'beyond a person's threshold and outside his [*sic*] possession' (Illich 1983, n.p.) – the woods or fields, for example, that secure a community's subsistence, protect it from flood and drought, and provide spiritual and aesthetic meaning. Instead, enclosure transforms the environment into a 'resource' for national or global production – into so many chips that can be cashed in as commodities, handed out as political favours and otherwise used to accrue influence.

Because it involves these and other equally visceral processes, the experience of enclosure – of accumulation by dispossession – is an experience that cannot be understood without first understanding the losses it entails, not in book-keeping terms but in terms of relationships. This is the crisis that is the proper starting point for a response to the 'what is to be done?' question (Sangkoyo 2015). Engaged with as a process of mutual discovery rather than as an exercise in rote empathy or stereotyping ('Pity the victim!' 'All hail the resister!'), it is a starting point that builds a very different 'We' to one that rushes into a 'to do' list. And, as it progresses, it opens up new questions and different perspectives on what activism might mean. For example:

> 'You tell me that the World Bank is responsible for this road: why then are you asking it to be part of the solution?'
>
> 'Why do we need to go to Washington to have a global impact? All the worst global forces are here. They are the cause of our crisis. We can confront them here. So why not come and join us?'
>
> 'Who is going to implement this list of policies that you have made? Why should we trust the government or companies or the development institutions to side with us? Why would they? Their cronyism does not offer the friendships we seek. We would like to explore more the questions of whose side are you on and what do you intend to do about it.'
>
> 'What you tell us about project bonds is very interesting and helps us understand more about who is doing this to us; but we would also like to talk about how we built our irrigation system without any money from the World Bank or private equity firms or capital markets.'
>
> 'Who is suffering from just-in-time delivery? How can we reach out to them?'
>
> 'What is this commons you talk about? Is it the same commons that the British talked about when they took away our lands "for the common good"? Would you like to hear about that history?'   (Goldtooth 2015)
>
> 'There is still much to discuss.'

And so on.

There is no shortcut around this slow, patient process of 'we-building' and, potentially, of class formation. But, for many activists, the talk of friendship as a political tool, let alone friendship as the political tool of the moment, is whimsy. It is as fanciful as the 'horticultural quietism' (to use the phrase of novelist Julian Barnes (2011)) recommended by Voltaire's Candide as the most practical response to the horrors that humans are capable of inflicting on each other ('Il faut cultiver notre jardin' – 'We must tend our own garden'). Most NGO colleagues would recognise the value of friendship in campaigning, but the notion that it might be an important goal *of* campaigning, let alone an organising principle *for* campaigning, would strike many as bizarre. As a tool for action, friendship may seem to cut no political ice. It may seem to lack the hard edge of reports, policy briefs, talking points, internet appeals and email bombardments.

Yet it is only within the space engendered by the patient, long-term building of relationships of trust that the process of discovery that is social justice can take place. It is only within this space that realistic strategies for breaking beyond what social philosopher André Gorz (1968) called 'reformist reforms' can emerge to embrace 'non-reformist reforms'. For an activism that gains maturity within this space is an activism rooted in the actual everyday struggles of people the world over to understand their oppression and to find ways around the obstacles that prevent *them* from creating the world *they* want. Where such activism is ignored, side-stepped or treated as a resource to be harnessed to campaigns that are conceived and put into practice outside of the process of social justice-as-discovery, the result is often to add to those obstacles, to the detriment of movement building.

6.3 In support of impolite politics

Creating spaces for 'patient' organising, and for evolving processes that would better encourage the sharing and exploration of loss, of recovery and of strategies for reweaving the friendships that make for commoning, is never easy; but, easy or not, it is where organising must surely root itself. It is the way that we live our lives both outside and inside of the world of paid labour, factories, corporations and state institutions; the way in which we become knowledgeable (Ingold 2010); it is the world in which we nurture children without pay, look after a neighbour, walk down busy streets without bumping into each other, or handle finance outside of formal banking institutions. Families would not function as families without commoning; the billions who earn less than $2 a day would not survive unless they 'gained some part of their subsistence using the commons' (Caffentzis 2009, p. 25); and capital itself would be considerably weakened if it was not able to rely on non-commodified forms of care (for instance, women's work in the home) to sustain its workforce.

But, at this time of flux and crisis, activists should be wary of assuming that political institutions that have served the commons well in the recent past can necessarily continue to provide an effective challenge to capital in the future. Recent years have seen the hollowing out of many of the cross-cutting, community-embedded networks of solidarity – from trade unions to working-class political parties – that have historically provided the seedbeds for building mutuality and challenging accumulation. In many countries, for example, trade unions are a vastly diminished political, social and economic force. To be clear, this is not to say that worker activism is diminished: the offshoring of European and US jobs to the global South may have weakened unions in Europe and the US, but it has simultaneously created new working-class movements in Asia, Latin America, China and elsewhere as labour militancy has erupted in response to oppressive factory conditions and the wider intrusions of capital (Silver 2003). And in Europe and the US, unions and union-led struggles continue. But notwithstanding such activism, the role that unions now play in society, particularly in the global North, has undoubtedly been weakened by neoliberal anti-union legislation; by the increased ability of capital to move around the world in search of cheaper labour; by changing patterns of production that make union organising more difficult; by the casualisation of labour; and by 'sectionalism' as unions have themselves shed some of their wider role in society to focus on bargaining over wages and conditions. Indeed, it is an open question whether unions as they now exist are 'capable of adequately responding to the scale of the problems working classes face – whether the arena of struggle is the workplace, the bargaining table, the community, electoral politics or ideological debate' (Gindin 2013, p. 26).

As the social science academic and activist John McDermott of the State University of New York argues, this hollowing out of labour's power may lie in a deeper historical shift that has seen 'the absorption, subordination and modification of virtually all of the more important general social relations into capitalist relations of production' (2007, p. 314). McDermott argues that part of what made labour powerful was its roots in social institutions, built by the working class themselves, that lay outside of what he terms 'polite society'. In the eighteenth and early nineteenth centuries, when working-class culture was being constructed through myriad relationships that brought an expanded awareness of oppression, working-class life went on 'more or less entirely outside society': unions, dissenting church groups, workers' clubs, reading groups, worker-run crèches, mutual aid societies and other cornerstones of working-class communities arose partly because wider society ignored working-class needs for schooling, healthcare and childcare. Rich and poor often occupied different, mutually hostile territories, with few shared political institutions or shared cultural activities or shared social infrastructure. To survive, workers were reliant on their own institutions and support networks. These were not only a response to the deprivations suffered: they were also a conscious attempt to build an 'alternate social and moral order'. Critically, this evolving working-class culture stood outside of 'Society'.

But between 1870 and 1970 working-class agitation for education, healthcare, liveable housing and social security converged dialectically with capital's emerging needs for better-educated, healthier workers. As more was invested in education and other social goods, so denser relationships developed between the classes, albeit with workers remaining subordinated. The working class have undoubtedly gained much from this in terms of improved standards of living but, argues McDermott, the development 'has not come about without important loss'. Many of the institutions of older working-class life have been undermined, weakened or eradicated; and those that survive are often now controlled by capitalist institutions. This may help to explain the weakening of labour's influence on society, since it was to a large degree the 'once semi-autonomous sources of working-class culture and cohesion' that provided labour with 'the base and fulcrum of its power' (McDermott 2007, pp. 318–19).

It may be anachronistic, however, to respond to crisis by trying to rebuild past institutions of working-class culture. Originally built 'outside of "polite" society', and with no expectation that 'polite society' would ever do more than stand in their way, they may not be fit as responses to the 'different, denser social terrain of the present' (McDermott 2007, p. 318). Instead, now that the 'infrastructure' of labour-power production built up between 1870 and 1970 is itself being dismantled and transformed under post-1970 neoliberalism, a more fruitful strategy may be to look to new, emerging forms and kinds of class conflict for clues to a transformative politics.

McDermott is confident that workers will do precisely this. And, indeed, in many instances they already are, whether in new forms of community-based solidarity with the struggles of unorganised labour (McAlevey 2015; Silver 2003), or in the many and varied forms of resistance pioneered by feminists to capitalist work (Federici 2012, 2013).

Other movements are also active in developing new forms of organising in the lattices created by the exclusion of working people from 'polite society', where 'the denser social terrain of the present' (McDermott 2007, p. 318) that has been woven over the past century is unravelling and fracturing. For it is in these lattices that 'impolite society' (if that is the appropriate term) is re-emerging to forge new cultures of provisioning, nurturing and mutual support to weather the destruction that the whirlwind of neoliberalism is inflicting. Although never entirely 'outside' of capital as a social order – it is doubtful that such a space exists – many of the experiments through which 'impolite' society is seeking to organise its own social reproduction are nonetheless outside some of the structures of capital (Caffentzis 2009) and, in an age when the interests of the state and capital are more closely aligned than at many times in the recent past, of the state itself. Such initiatives include community-supported agriculture; land and factory occupations; credit unions; the teaming-up of unions with communities or local municipalities to finance and build socially owned renewable energy schemes (Abramsky 2014) or social housing; and the setting-up of solidarity health clinics in response to the slashing of public health budgets. Another example is the region-wide experiment in 'stateless democracy' by the Kurds of war-torn Syria and south-east Turkey to put their demands for autonomy into practice by setting up a web of village and municipal councils through which they can govern themselves – formulating their own laws, building their own universities, creating their own parliaments – regardless of the parallel existence of the Turkish and Syrian states that have for so long brutally repressed their aspirations (TATORT Kurdistan 2013; New World Academy 2015).

Each of these experiments in creating 'impolite' polities is unique. They cannot be packaged into a modular form that can be reproduced and assembled anywhere, for the friendships on which they are built are not mechanically replicable Meccano pieces. They are built by commoning born of place, historical context and specific experiences. To treat them as 'models' is to miss the essence of what makes them work. But they can act as inspirations – as what writer and activist John Holloway calls 'flashes, intimations, anticipations, fragments of the world of dignity that we want to create' (2009, p. xvii). They can be supported through the cross-fertilisation of ideas, the exchange of experiences and respectful solidarity. These 'societies in movement' (Zibechi 2010, p. 76) are where the most promising vectors for transformative change will be found. Rather than looking for a 'to do' list that will be implemented by someone else, they are building their own power 'to do', a process that involves 'modify[ing] the relationship of forces, the redistribution of functions and powers, [while introducing] new centers of democratic decision-making' (Gorz 1968, p. 58). That struggle is no longer primarily within polite society: rather it is increasingly once again outside of society. It is surely here, and only here, that the elements of another world can best be built, relationship by patiently nurtured relationship. And those relationships may well start not with conversations about 'infrastructure' or 'finance' or 'commons' or 'capital', still less with 'give me a list for my campaign', but with the often incoherent, always painful, gropings for an explanation of crisis, loss and injustice.

Note

1 'Activism' is used here to capture any action that is intended to unsettle and change the status quo – and thus encompasses a wide range of activities, from, say, a discussion between friends on 'what is wrong' to a demonstration against a human rights abuse to the act of caring for a neighbour. Activists are not just those concerned with social justice. Bankers and private equity fund managers also see themselves as activists when seeking to change the status quo of a regulation or the management of a firm. 'Organising' is about activism gaining strategy and tactics.

References

4–Traders (2015) 'Netcare'. Available at: http://www.4–traders. com/NETCARE-LIMITED-1413397/company/ (accessed August 2015).

Abramsky, K. (2014) 'Building a socially-owned renewable energy sector' in N. Hildyard and L. Lohmann, *Energy, Work and Finance*. Sturminster Newton, Dorset: The Corner House, 86. Available at: http://www.thecornerhouse.org.uk/sites/thecornerhouse.org. uk/files/EnergyWorkFinance%20%282.57MB%29.pdf (accessed November 2015).

ACCA (Association of Certified Chartered Accountants) (2012) *Taking Stock of PPP and PFI Around the World*. Research Report 126. London: Certified Accountants Educational Trust. Available at: http://www.accaglobal.com/content/dam/acca/global/PDF-technical/public-sector/rr-126–001.pdf (accessed August 2015).

Actis (2012) 'Actis in review 2012'. Available at: http://www.act.is/ ActisPDFs/ActisInReview2012.pdf (accessed August 2015).

ADB/ADBI (Asian Development Bank and Asian Development Bank Institute) (2009) *Infrastructure for a Seamless Asia*. Available at: http://adb.org/sites/default/files/pub/2009/2009.08.31.book.infra structure.seamless.asia.pdf (accessed September 2015).

Allen, J. and Pryke, M. (2013) 'Financializing household water: Thames Water, MEIF, and "ring-fenced" politics'. *Cambridge Journal of Regions, Economy and Society* 6(3): 419–39 (online). Available at: http://cjres.oxfordjournals.org/content/6/3/419.full (accessed August 2015).

Antropov, D. and Perarnaud, J. (2013) *Emerging Markets Infrastructure: Risk, Returns and Current Opportunities*. Partners Group Research Flash, October 2013. Available at: http:// www.partnersgroup.com/fileadmin/user_upload/Content_PDFs/ documents/Research_Flashes_PDF/201310_INFRA_Emerging_ markets_infrastructure_-_risk__returns_and_current_opportuni ties.pdf (accessed June 2014).

Arce, L. (2009) 'Peru: Massive protests against García government over Amazon massacre'. *World Socialist Website*, 13 June 2009. Available at: https://www.wsws.org/en/articles/2009/06/peru-j13. html (accessed September 2015).

ASEAN (Association of Southeast Asian Nations) (2010) *Masterplan on ASEAN Connectivity: One Vision, One Identity, One Community*. Jakarta: ASEAN. Available at: http://investasean.asean.org/index. php/ajax/exec_ajax/file_download/824/newsid/966/master-plan-on-asean-connectivity.pdf (accessed September 2015).

Aslan, C. (2014) *How Do Countries Measure, Manage and Monitor Fiscal Risks Generated by Public Private Partnerships? Chile, Peru, South Africa, Turkey*. Washington, DC: The Treasury, World Bank. Available at: http://www.worldbank.org/content/ dam/Worldbank/document/Debt/Presentation%20Cigdem%20 New%20Avenues.pdf (accessed 2 March 2016).

Assegaf, I. and Wiriasmoko, Y. (2013) 'Indonesia: An economic masterplan'. *International Financial Law Review*, 13 January 2013. Available at: http://www.iflr.com/Article/3130827/Indonesia-An-economic-masterplan.html (accessed September 2015).

AwasMIFEE (2015) 'MIFEE and other top-down developments in Papua will continue under Jokowi administration'. Available at: https://awasmifee.potager.org/?p=1127 (accessed September 2015).

Baker, D. (2011) *The Origins and Severity of the Public Pension Crisis*. Washington, DC: Center for Economic and Policy Research. Available at: http://www.cepr.net/documents/publica tions/pensions-2011–02.pdf (accessed August 2015).

Bappenas (National Development Planning Agency Indonesia) (2011) 'National connectivity 2011 Special Edition'. *Sustaining Partnership*. Available at: http://pkps.bappenas.go.id/attachments/ article/957/DESEMBER%20Khusus_KONEKTIFITAS_ENG LISH_L.pdf (accessed September 2015).

Barbero, J.A. (2011) *Infrastructure in the Comprehensive Development of Latin America: Strategic Diagnosis and Proposals for a Priority Agenda, IDeAL 2011*. Caracas: CAF (Corporación Andina de Fomento) Available at: http://publicaciones.caf.com/ media/17158/infraestructure_in_the_comprehensive_developme nt.pdf (accessed September 2015).

Barnes, J. (2011) 'A candid view of Candide'. *Guardian*, 1 July 2011. Available at: http://www.theguardian.com/books/2011/jul/01/can dide-voltaire-rereading-julian-barnes (accessed November 2015).

Bayliss, K. (2014) *Case Study: The Financialisation of Water in England and Wales*. FESSUD (Financialisation, Economy, Society and

Sustainable Development) Working Paper Series No. 52. Available at: http://fessud.eu/wp-content/uploads/2015/03/Case-study-the-financialisation-of-Water-in-England-and-Wales-Bayliss-working-paper-REVISED_annexes-working-paper-52.pdf (accessed July 2015).

Beeferman, L.W. (2008) *Pension Fund Investment in Infrastructure: A Resource Paper.* Occasional Paper Series, No. 3. Cambridge, MA: Pensions and Capital Stewardship Project Labor and Worklife Program, Harvard Law School. Available at: http://www.law.harvard.edu/programs/lwp/pensions/publications/occpapers/occasionalpapers3.pdf (accessed July 2015).

Beira Corridor (undated) *Beira Agricultural Growth Corridor: Delivering the Potential.* Available at: http://www.agdevco.com/sysimages/BAGC_Investment_Blueprint.pdf (accessed September 2015).

Blanc-Brude, F. (2014) *Benchmarking Long-Term Investment in Infrastructure: Objectives, Roadmap and Recent Progress.* Singapore: EDHEC Risk Institute-Asia. Available at: http://www.edhec-risk.com/edhec_publications/all_publications/RISK Review.2014–06–18.1812/attachments/EDHEC_Position_Paper_Benchmarking_Long_Term_Investment_in_Infrastructure.pdf (accessed July 2015).

Bogart, D. and Chaudhary, L. (2012), *Railways in Colonial India: An Economic Achievement?* Available at: http://www.socsci.uci.edu/~dbogart/railwaysahievjune2012.pdf (accessed June 2015).

Boston University (2013) *Endline Study for Queen 'Mamohato Hospital Public Private Partnership (PPP).* Available at: http://devpolicy.org/pdf/Endline-Study-PPP-Lesotho-Final-Report-2013.pdf (accessed August 2015).

Brennan, J. (2015) *Ascent of Giants: NAFTA, Corporate Power and the Growing Income Gap.* Ottawa, Ontario: Canadian Centre for Policy Alternatives. Available at: https://www.policyalternatives.ca/publications/reports/ascent-giants (accessed April 2015).

Brenner, N. (2014) 'Urban governance – at what scale?' *LSECities.* Available at: https://lsecities.net/media/objects/articles/urban-governance-at-what-scale/en-gb/ (accessed September 2015).

Brunner, H.-P. (2013) 'What is economic corridor development and what can it achieve in Asia's subregions?' ADB Working Paper Series on Regional Economic Integration 117. Manila: Asian Development Bank. Available at: http://www10.iadb.org/intal/intalcdi/PE/2013/12562.pdf (accessed September 2015).

Bunker, S.G. and Ciccantell, P.S. (2005) *Globalization and the Race for Resources*. Baltimore. MD: Johns Hopkins University Press.

Caffentzis, G. (2009) 'The future of the "commons": neoliberalism's "Plan B" or the original disaccumulation of capital?' *New Formations* 69: 23–41. Available at: https://newxcommoners.files. wordpress.com/2013/01/caffentzis-planb.pdf (accessed October 2015).

Caffentzis, G. (2012) 'A tale of two conferences: globalization, the crisis of neoliberalism and question of the commons'. *Borderlands* 11(2): 1–32.

Che, J. (2015) 'Here's how outrageous the pay gap between CEOs and workers is'. *Huffington Post*, 27 August 2015. Available at: http://www.huffingtonpost.com/entry/ceo-worker-pay-gap_55ddc3c7e4b0a40aa3acd1c9 (accessed November 2015).

Communique of Brasilia (2000). 1 September 2000. Available at: http://go.usa.gov/3pJYC (accessed September 2015).

Consulate General of India (2014) 'India: The Investment Destination' in Kegler Brown Hill + Ritter, 'Succeeding in India: business + legal insights'. Slide presentation. Available at: http://www.slideshare. net/KeglerBrown/succeeding-in-india (accessed September 2015).

Cook, P. and Uchida, Y. (2004) *An Appraisal of the Performance of Privatized Enterprises in Developing Countries*. Working Paper Series Paper No. 105. Manchester: Centre on Regulation and Competition, University of Manchester. Available at: http://r4d. dfid.gov.uk/PDF/Outputs/RegComp/CRCwp105.pdf (accessed July 2015).

CSE India (2011) 'Water PPPs: are they here to stay?' New Delhi: Centre for Science and Environment India. Available at: http:// www.cseindia.org/userfiles/fullstory_final.pdf (accessed August 2015).

Dannin, E. (2011) 'Crumbling infrastructure, crumbling democracy: infrastructure privatization contracts and their effects on state and local governance'. *Northwestern Journal of Law and Social Policy* 6(1): 47–105. Available at: http://scholarlycommons.law.northwestern.edu/cgi/viewcontent.cgi?article=1061&context=njlsp (accessed August 2015).

Della Croce, R. and Yermo, J. (2013) 'Institutional investors and infrastructure financing'. OECD Working Papers on Finance, Insurance and Private Pensions, No. 36. Paris: OECD Publishing. Available at: http://www.mmc.com/content/dam/mmc-web/Files/ OECD-Institutional-investors-and-Infrastructure-financing-Working-Paper-No-36.pdf (accessed August 2015).

di Borgo, P. (2012) *Shared Mining Infrastructure: Too Good to be True? Trends, Challenges and Opportunities for Private Financing of Mining-Associated Transport Infrastructure in SSA.* Washington, DC: IFC. Available at: http://www.worldbank.org/content/dam/Worldbank/document/Extractives/Mining%20Indaba%202014/Pierre%20Pozzo%20di%20Borgo%20INdaba%202014%20Presentation%20v2.pdf (accessed September 2015).

DMICDC (Delhi Mumbai Industrial Corridor Development Corporation) (2015) 'Welcome to DMICDC'. Available at: http://www.dmicdc.com/Default.aspx (accessed September 2015).

Dobbs, R., Remes, J., Manyika, J., Roxburgh, C., Smit, S. and Schaer, F. (2012) *Urban World: Cities and the Rise of the Consuming Class.* McKinsey Global Institute. Available at: http://www.mckinsey.com/insights/urbanization/urban_world_cities_and_the_rise_of_the_consuming_class (accessed September 2015).

Dobbs, R., Manyika, J. and Woetzel, J. (2015) 'The four global forces breaking all the trends'. McKinsey Global Institute. Available at: http://www.mckinsey.com/insights/strategy/the_four_global_forces_breaking_all_the_trends (accessed September 2015).

Dorling, D. (2010) *Injustice: Why Social Inequality Persists.* Bristol: Policy Press.

The Economist (2014a) 'Piketty fever: Bigger than Marx'. 3 May 2014. Available at: http://www.economist.com/news/finance-and-economics/21601567–wonky-book-inequality-becomes-blockbuster-bigger-marx (accessed April 2015).

The Economist (2014b) 'The New Silk Road: Hardly an oasis'. 13 November 2014. Available at: http://www.economist.com/news/asia/21632595–kazakhstan-turns-geography-advantage-china-builds-new-silk-road-hardly-oasis (accessed September 2015).

EIU (2015) *Prospects and Challenges on China's 'One Belt, One Road': A Risk Assessment.* Available at: http://www.eiu.com/public/topical_report.aspx?campaignid=OneBeltOneRoad (accessed September 2015).

Elmer, V. and Leigland, A. (2014) *Infrastructure Planning and Finance: A Smart and Sustainable Guide.* New York: Routledge.

Elstrodt, H.-P., Manyika, J., Remes, J., Ellen, P. and Martins, C. (2014) *Connecting Brazil to the World: A Path to Inclusive Growth.* McKinsey Global Institute. Available at: http://www.mckinsey.com/~/media/McKinsey/Global%20Themes/Americas/Brazils%20path%20to%20inclusive%20growth/MGI_Connecting_Brazil_to_the_world_Full_report_May%202014.ashx

Engelen, E. and Williams, K. (2014) 'Commentary: Just the facts: on the success of Piketty's *Capital*'. *Environment and Planning A* 46: 1771–7. Available at: http://www.envplan.com/openaccess/a474c.pdf (accessed April 2015).

Esteva, G. (2013) 'Aid – No thanks! If anyone wants to do you any good, run away'. Presentation to 'Giornata di dialogo tra movimenti', Florence, 8 April 2013.

Esteva, G. (2014) 'Commoning in the new society'. *Community Development Journal* 49 (suppl 1): i144–i159. Available at: http://cdj.oxfordjournals.org/content/49/suppl_1/i144.full (accessed November 2015).

European Commission (2015a) 'An illustrative project example: Europe 2020 project bond initiative'. DG Economic and Financial Affairs. Available at: http://ec.europa.eu/economy_finance/financial_operations/investment/europe_2020/project_example_en.htm (accessed August 2015).

European Commission (2015b) 'New EU rules to promote investment in infrastructure projects'. Brussels: European Commission. Available at: http://europa.eu/rapid/press-release_MEMO-15–5734_fr.htm (accessed October 2015).

Faustino Coelho, C. and O'Farrell, C. (2009) 'Breaking new ground: Lesotho hospital public–private partnership – a model for integrated health services delivery'. *IFCSmartLessons*. Available at: http://www.ifc.org/wps/wcm/connect/72379880498390c582f4d2336b93d75f/LesothoHospital_Smartlesson.pdf?MOD=AJPERES (accessed August 2015).

Favas, M. (2014) 'What the numbers really mean'. *Infrastructure Investor*, 28 February 2014. Available at: http://georginderst.com/resources/PEI+II+Mar+2014+Whatthenumbersreallymean.pdf (accessed August 2015).

Favas, M. (2015a) 'Not so lonely at the top'. *Infrastructure Investor*, 29 January 2015. Available at: https://www.infrastructureinvestor.com/Free_Articles/Not_so_lonely_at_the_top/ (accessed August 2015).

Favas, M. (2015b) 'Week in review: Partners in prime'. *Infrastructure Investor*, 11 June 2015.

Federici, S. (2011) 'A feminist critique of Marx'. *End of Capitalism*, 29 May 2013. Available at: http://endofcapitalism.com/2013/05/29/a-feminist-critique-of-marx-by-silvia-federici/ (accessed November 2015).

Federici, S. (ed.) (2012) *Revolution at Point Zero*. Oakland, CA: PM Press.

Firman, V. and Litlhakanyane, V. (2010) *Public Private Partnerships*. Netcare Investor. Available at: http://www.netcareinvestor.co.za/ pdf/presentations/lesotho_ppp_sept_2010.pdf (accessed August 2015).

Foster, V. (2008) *Overhauling the Engine of Growth: Infrastructure in Africa*. Washington, DC: Africa Infrastructure Country Diagnostic, World Bank. Available at: http://siteresources.worldbank. org/INTAFRICA/Resources/AICD_exec_summ_9–30–08a.pdf (accessed September 2015).

Friedman, T.L. (2012) 'Made in the world'. *New York Times*, 28 January 2012. Available at: http://www.nytimes.com/2012/01/29/ opinion/sunday/friedman-made-in-the-world.html?_r=0 (accessed September 2015).

Friedman-Rudovsky, J. (2012) 'The bully from Brazil'. *Foreign Policy*, 20 July 2012. Available at: http://foreignpolicy.com/2012/07/20/ the-bully-from-brazil/?wp_login_redirect=0 (accessed September 2015)

Froud, J., Johal, S., Leaver, A. and Williams, K. (2012) *Apple Business Model: Financialization across the Pacific*. CRESC Working Paper No. 111. Milton Keynes and Manchester: CRESC. Available at: http://www.cresc.ac.uk/medialibrary/workingpapers/ wp111.pdf (accessed April 2015).

Gindin, S. (2013) 'Rethinking unions, registering socialism'. *Socialist Register 2013*, 26–51.

Global Infrastructure Basel (2015) *5th GIB Summit 27–18 May 2015 Report*. Basel: Global Infrastructure Basel. Available at: http://www.gib-foundation.org/content/uploads/2015/07/5th-GIB-Summit-Report.pdf (accessed July 2015).

Goldtooth, T. (2015) 'About commons, crisis and the inheritance of loss' in *Commoning as a Political Act: Conversations from Collevecchio*. Sturminster Newton, Dorset: The Corner House and Rome: Re:Common.

Gorz, A. (1968) *Strategy for Labor: A Radical Proposal*. Boston: Beacon Press.

Government of Turkey (1999) *Host Government Agreement Between and Among the Government of the Republic of Turkey and the [MEP Participants]*. Available at: http://subsites.bp.com/ caspian/BTC/Eng/agmt3/agmt3.PDF (accessed September 2015).

Grappi, G. (2015) 'Logistics, infrastructures and governance after Piraeus: Notes on logistical worlds'. *Logistical Worlds: Infrastructure, Software, Labour*, 4 August 2015. Available at: http://logisticalworlds.org/blogs/logistics-infrastructures-and-governance-after-piraeus-notes-on-logistical-worlds#more-383 (accessed September 2015).

Green, S. (2013) 'Made in the world'. *OECD Observer*, No. 296, Q1 2013. Available at: http://www.oecd.org/innovation/made-in-the-world.htm (accessed September 2015).

Guttal, S. (2014) 'Pursuing privatization: the ADB's unchanging vision of development'. *Focus on the Global South*. Available at: http://focusweb.org/content/pursuing-privatization-adbs-unchanging-vision-development (accessed September 2015).

Hall, D. (2007) *Energy Privatization and Reform in East Africa*. London: Public Services International Research Unit. Available at: http://www.psiru.org/reports/2006–11–E-Eafrica.doc (accessed August 2015).

Hall, D. (2015) *Why Public–Private Partnerships Don't Work: The Many Advantages of the Public Alternative*. London: Public Services International Research Unit. Available at: http://www.psiru.org/sites/default/files/2015–03–PPP-WhyPPPsdontworkEng.pdf (accessed July 2015).

Hall, D. and Lobina, E. (2006) *Pipe Dreams: The Failure of the Private Sector to Invest in Water Services in Developing Countries*. London: Public Services International Research Unit; Ferney-Voltaire Cedex: Public Services International; and London: World Development Movement. Available at: http://gala.gre.ac.uk/3601/1/PSIRU_9618_-_2006–03–W-investment.pdf (accessed July 2015).

Hall, D. and Lobina, E. (2008) *Water Privatisation*. London: Public Services International Research Unit. Available at: http://gala.gre.ac.uk/1704/1/PSIRU_Report_%289820%29_-_2008–04–W-over.pdf (accessed July 2015).

Harvey, D. (1989) *The Condition of Postmodernity: An Enquiry into the Origins of Cultural Change*. Oxford: Blackwell.

Harvey, D. (1990) 'Between space and time: reflections on the geographical imagination'. *Annals of the Association of American Geographers* 80(3): 418–34. Available at: http://isites.harvard.edu/fs/docs/icb.topic80806.files/Week_6/Harvey_D_Between_Space_and_Time.pdf (accessed September 2015).

Harvey, D. (2001) *Spaces of Capital: Towards a Critical Geography*. New York: Routledge.

Harvey, D. (2004) 'The "new" imperialism: accumulation by dispossession'. *Socialist Register 2004*, 63–87. Available at: http://socialistregister.com/index.php/srv/article/view/5811/2707#.Vh AiaZc3f2g (accessed September 2015).

Harvey, D. (2008) 'David Harvey on the geography of capitalism: understanding cities as polities and shifting imperialisms'. *Theory Talks #20: David Harvey*. Available at: http://www.theory-talks.org/2008/10/theory-talk-20–david-harvey.html (accessed November 2015).

Harvey, D. (2014) 'Afterthoughts on Piketty's *Capital*'. Available at: http://davidharvey.org/2014/05/afterthoughts-pikettys-capital/ (accessed April 2015).

High Court of South Africa (2015) *In the matter between Netcare Hospital Group (PTY) Ltd and Afri'nnai Health PTY Ltd and Five Others: Judgment*. 26 February 2015. Available at: http://www.saflii.org/za/cases/ZAFSHC/2015/40.html (accessed August 2015).

Hilary, J. (2104) *The Transatlantic Trade and Investment Partnership: A Charter for Deregulation, An Attack on Jobs, An End to Democracy*. London: War on Want and Brussels: Rosa-Luxemburg-Stiftung. Available at: http://www.waronwant.org/attachments/HILARY_LONDON_FINAL_WEB.pdf (accessed April 2015).

Hildyard, N. (2008) *A (Crumbling) Wall of Money: Financial Bricolage, Derivatives and Power*. Corner House Briefing 39. Available at: http://www.thecornerhouse.org.uk/resource/crumb ling-wall-money (accessed October 2015).

Hildyard, N. (2012) *More than Bricks and Mortar: Infrastructure-as-Asset-Class: Financing Development or Developing Finance?* Sturminster Newton, Dorset: The Corner House. Available at: http://www.thecornerhouse.org.uk/sites/thecornerhouse.org.uk/files/Bricks%20and%20Mortar.pdf (accessed June 2015).

Hildyard, N. (2015) *Global Looting – A Snap Shot*. Sturminster Newton, Dorset: The Corner House. Available at: http://www.thecornerhouse.org.uk/resource/global-looting-snap-shot (accessed November 2015).

Hildyard, N. and Lohmann, L. (2013) *The Museum of Fetishes*. Sturminster Newton, Dorset: The Corner House. Available at: http://www.thecornerhouse.org.uk/sites/thecornerhouse.org.uk/files/The%20Museum%20of%20Fetishes.pdf (accessed September 2015).

Hildyard, N. and Lohmann, L. (2014) *Energy, Work and Finance*. Sturminster Newton, Dorset: The Corner House. Available at: http://www.thecornerhouse.org.uk/sites/thecornerhouse.org.uk/files/EnergyWorkFinance%20%282.57MB%29.pdf.

Hildyard, N. and Muttitt, G. (2006) 'Turbo-charging investor sovereignty: investment agreements and corporate colonialism' in

Focus on the Global South, *Destroy and Profit: Wars, Disasters and Corporations*. Bangkok: Focus on the Global South, 43–63. Available at: http://www.focusweb.org/pdf/Reconstruction-Dossier.pdf (accessed August 2015).

HM Treasury (2012) *Standardisation of PF2 Contracts*. London: HM Treasury. Available at: https://www.gov.uk/government/uploads/system/uploads/attachment_data/file/221556/infrastructure_standardisation_of_contracts_051212.pdf (accessed August 2015).

Holloway, J. (2009) 'Foreword to the German Edition' in R. Zibechi, *Dispersing Power: Social Movements as Anti-State Forces*. Oakland, CA: AK Press.

Hudgins, M. and Sharma, P. (2014) *Accessing Asia: Investing in the Infrastructure Imperative*. Investment Insights series. New York: JP Morgan Asset Management. Available at: https://am.jpmorgan.com/blobcontent/1383199916775/83456/II_Accessing_Asia_infrastructure_imperative.pdf (accessed August 2014).

Hyde, P., Burns, D., Hassard, J. and Killett, A. (2014) 'Colonizing the aged body and the organization of later life'. *Organization Studies* 35(11): 1699–717. Available at: http://dro.dur.ac.uk/12984/1/12984.pdf?DDD2+rsjf35+dul4eg (accessed August 2015).

ICSID (2010) *In the proceedings between Suez, Sociedad General de Aguas de Barcelona S.A., and Vivendi Universal S.A. (Claimants) and The Argentine Republic (Respondent): Decision on Liability*. ICSID Case No. ARB/03/19. Washington, DC: International Centre for Settlement of Investment Disputes. Available at: http://www.italaw.com/documents/SuezVivendiAWGDeciciononLiability.pdf (accessed August 2015).

IFC (International Finance Corporation) (2013) *Fostering the Development of Greenfield Mining-Related Transport Infrastructure through Project Financing*. Washington, DC: Public–Private Infrastructure Advisory Facility (PPIAF) and World Bank. Available at: http://www.ifc.org/wps/wcm/connect/c019bf004f4c6ebfbd99ff032730e94e/Mine+Infra+Report+Final+Copy.pdf?MOD=AJPERES (accessed September 2015).

IIRSA (2011) *IIRSA: 10 Years Later – Achievements and Challenges*. Available at: http://www.iirsa.org/admin_iirsa_web/Uploads/Documents/lb_iirsa_10_anios_sus_logros_y_desafios_eng.pdf (accessed September 2015).

IIRSA (2014a) 'The Portfolio in Figures'. Available at: http://www.iirsa.org/Page/Detail?menuItemId=72 (accessed September 2015).

IIRSA (2014b) *Integration Priority Project Agenda: Progress Report*. Available at: http://www.iirsa.org/admin_iirsa_web/

Uploads/Documents/api_informe_avance_2014_eng.pdf (accessed September 2015).

IIRSA (2015) *Proyectos Concluidos de la Cartera del COSIPLAN*. Available at: http://www.iirsa.org/admin_iirsa_web/Uploads/Documents/cartera_montevideo15_Presentacion_CARTERA_DE_PROYECTOS_CONCLUIDOS_v13–04_anexo7.pdf (accessed September 2015).

Illich, I. (1982) *Gender*. New York: Pantheon.

Illich, I. (1983) 'Silence is a commons'. *The Coevolution Quarterly*, Winter 1983. Available at: http://www.preservenet.com/theory/Illich/Silence.html (accessed November 2015).

Illich, I. (1996) 'Ivan Illich with Jerry Brown: We the People, KPFA'. Available at: http://www.wtp.org/archive/transcripts/ivan_illich_jerry.html (accessed November 2015).

IMF (2006) *Public–Private Partnerships, Government Guarantees, and Fiscal Risk*. Washington, DC: International Monetary Fund. Available at: https://www.imf.org/External/Pubs/NFT/2006/ppp/eng/ppp.pdf (accessed August 2015).

Inderst, G. (2009) 'Pension fund investment in infrastructure'. OECD Working Paper on Insurance and Private Pensions No. 32. Paris: OECD Publishing. Available at: http://www.oecd.org/finance/private-pensions/42052208.pdf (accessed July 2015).

Inderst, G. (2010) 'Infrastructure as an asset class'. *EIB Papers* 15(1): 70–104. Available at: http://www.pensions-institute.org/workingpapers/wp1103.pdf (accessed July 2015).

Inderst, G. (2013) *Private Infrastructure Finance and Investment in Europe*. EIB Working Papers 2013/02. Luxembourg: European Investment Bank. Available at: http://www.eib.org/attachments/efs/economics_working_paper_2013_02_en.pdf (accessed July 2015).

Inderst, G. and Stewart, F. (2014) *Institutional Investment in Infrastructure in Developing Countries: Introduction to Potential Models*. Policy Research Working Paper 6780. Washington, DC: World Bank. Available at: https://openknowledge.worldbank.org/bitstream/handle/10986/18358/WPS6780.pdf?sequence=1 (accessed July 2015).

Infrastructure Investor (2010) 'Week in review: hope springs eternal'. 28 October 2010.

Ingold, T. (2010) 'Footprint through the weather-world: walking, breathing, knowing'. *Journal of Royal Anthropological Institute* (N.S.): S121–S139.

IPA (Indian Ports Association) (2007) *Coordination of Business Plans for Major Ports in India: Consolidated Port Development*

Plan. Report prepared by Port of Rotterdam Authority, Vol. 1. Available at: http://ipa.nic.in/Definitief%20Volume%201.pdf (accessed September 2015).

Irwin, T.C. (2007) *Government Guarantees: Allocating and Valuing Risk in Privately Financed Infrastructure Projects*. Washington, DC: World Bank. Available at: http://siteresources.worldbank. org/INTSDNETWORK/Resources/Government_Guarantees.pdf (accessed August 2015).

Jack, I. (2014) 'Britain took more out of India than it put in – could China do the same to Britain?' *Guardian*, 20 June 2014. Available at: http://www.theguardian.com/commentisfree/2014/jun/20/brit ain-took-more-out-of-india (accessed June 2015).

Jaramillo, P. (2015) 'The Latin American infrastructure pipeline' in Norton Rose Fulbright (ed.) *Nexus: A Global Infrastructure Resource*, 50–7. Available at: http://www.nortonrosefulbright. com/files/nexus-127549.pdf#page=50 (accessed September 2015).

Kaarhus, R. (2011) *Agricultural Growth Corridors Equals Land-grabbing? Models, Roles and Accountabilities in a Mozambican case*. Paper presented at the International Conference on Global Land Grabbing, 6–8 April 2011. Land Deal Politics Initiative. The Hague: International Institute of Social Studies. Available at: http://www.iss.nl/fileadmin/ASSETS/iss/Documents/Conference_ papers/LDPI/76_Randi_Kaarhus.pdf (accessed September 2015).

Kabi, P. (2015a) 'Netcare accused of "bleeding" Tšepong Consortium'. *Public Eye Online*, 26 June 2015. Available at: http://www.publiceyenews.com/site/2015/06/26/netcare-accused- of-bleeding-tsepong-consortium/ (accessed August 2015).

Kabi, P. (2015b) 'Netcare seeks hostile buyout'. *Public Eye Online*, 7 August 2015. Available at: http://www.publiceyenews.com/ site/2015/08/07/netcare-seeks-hostile-buyout/ (accessed August 2015).

Kaminska, I. (2015) 'China's defence against supply chain disrup-tion'. *FT Alphaville*, 5 June 2015. Available at: http://ftalphaville. ft.com/2015/06/05/2131157/chinas-defence-against-supply-chain- disruption/ (accessed September 2015).

Kessides, I.N. (2004) *Reforming Infrastructure: Privatization, Regulation, and Competition*. Washington, DC: World Bank and Oxford University Press. Available at: https://openknowledge. worldbank.org/bitstream/handle/10986/13525/289850PAPER0re forming0infrastructure.pdf?sequence=1 (accessed July 2015).

Khaketla, M. (2015) 'Bringing back hope: budget speech to the parliament'. Minister of Finance, Government of Lesotho, 11

May 2015. Available at: http://www.lra.org.ls/Downloadable_
Docs/Adverts/LESOTHO%20GOVERNMENT%20%20–%20
2015%20BUDGET%20SPEECH%20–%20MINISTER%20
OF%20FINANCE.pdf?FileID=32662 (accessed August 2015).

Kim, J-H., Kim, J., Shin, S. and Lee, S-Y (2011) *Public–Private Partnership Infrastructure Projects: Case Studies from the Republic of Korea, Volume 1: Institutional Arrangements and Performance.* Mandaluyong City: Asian Development Bank. Available at: http://www.adb.org/sites/default/files/publication/29032/ppp-kor-v1.pdf (accessed August 2015).

KPMG (2014) *Infrastructure 100: World Markets Report.* Available at: https://www.kpmg.com/Global/en/IssuesAndInsights/Articles Publications/infra100–world-markets/Documents/infrastructure-100–world-markets-report-v3.pdf (accessed July 2015).

Kranc, J. (2014) 'Separating the wheat from the chaff'. *Infrastructure Investor: Emerging Markets Handbook*, June 2014.

Kumar, R. (2015) 'Delhi Mumbai Corridor: how the world's largest infrastructure project is uprooting Indian farmers'. *Guardian*, 15 September 2015. Available at: http://www.theguardian.com/cities/2015/sep/15/indias-future-dmic-delhi-mumbai-industrial-corridor (accessed September 2015).

Kunaka, C. (2011) *Maputo Development Corridor.* Washington, DC: World Bank. Available at: http://www.carecprogram.org/uploads/events/2011/SOM-Nov/Maputo-Development-Corridor.pdf (accessed September 2015).

Kunkel, B. (2014) 'Paupers and richlings'. *London Review of Books* 36(13): 17–20. Available at: http://www.lrb.co.uk/v36/n13/benjamin-kunkel/paupers-and-richlings (accessed April 2015).

LAWR *(Latin America Weekly Report)* (2009) 'Garcia's development plans trigger bloody clashes in Peru's Amazon'. *Latin America Weekly Report*, 11 June 2009, 1–2. Available at: http://www.latinnews.com/media/k2/pdf/gdptbcipa.pdf (accessed September 2015).

Lehmacher, W. and Padilla-Taylor, V. (2015) 'Hurdles along the "New Silk Road"'. *Financial Times*, 17 September 2015.

Lesotho Court of Appeal (2013) *Excel Health (Pty) Ltd v Dr Teboho Masia and Others: Judgment.* Available at: http://www.lesotholii.org/files/ls/judgment/court-appeal/2013/6/april_2013_excel_health_pty_ltd_v_dr_teboho_masia_43945.doc (accessed August 2015).

Lewis, C. M. (1983) *British Railways in Argentina 1857–1914: A Case Study of Foreign Investment.* Monograph 12. London:

University of London Institute of Latin American Studies. Cited in Irwin (2007, p. 2).

Leys, C. (2001) *Market-Driven Politics: Neoliberal Democracy and the Public Interest*. London: Verso.

Linebaugh, P. (2008) *The Magna Carta Manifesto: Liberties and Commons for all*. Berkeley, CA: University of California Press.

Lister, J. (2011) 'Lesotho hospital public private partnership: new model or false start?' *Global Health Check*, 16 December 2011. Available at: http://www.globalhealthcheck.org/?p=481 (accessed August 2015).

Live-Counter (2015) 'Bill Gates money counter'. Available at: http://www.live-counter.com/bill-gates-money-counter/ (accessed March 2015).

Lohmann, L. (2015a) 'What is the "green" in "green growth"?' in G. Dale, M.V. Mathai and J.A. Puppim de Oliveira (eds) *Green Growth: Political Ideology, Political Economy and Policy Alternatives*. London: Zed Books (forthcoming).

Lohmann, L. (2015b) 'Justice matters'. *Testimonies of Justice*. The Global Environmental Justice Group, School of International Development University of East Anglia. Available at: https://www.youtube.com/watch?v=8hMmr4rgMWk&list=PL2tuXXfyo5WSt6fH9uM6e5oomAcLQiBFR&index=18; transcript available at: http://www.thecornerhouse.org.uk/sites/thecornerhouse.org.uk/files/JusticeMattersCornerHouse.pdf (accessed November 2015).

Lohmann, L. (2015c) 'Reflections on Rimaflow'. Sturminster Newton, Dorset: The Corner House and Rome: Re:Common.

Lorenzen, C., Barrientos, M. with Babbar, S. (2001) *Toll Road Concessions: The Chilean Experience*. PFG Discussion Paper Series, No. 124. Washington, DC: World Bank. Available at: http://siteresources.worldbank.org/INTGUARANTEES/Resources/TollRoads_Concessions.pdf (accessed August 2015).

Luxemburg, R. (2003) [1951] *The Accumulation of Capital*. London and New York: Routledge. Available in the original at: https://www.marxists.org/archive/luxemburg/1913/accumulation-capital/accumulation.pdf (accessed September 2015).

Manyika, J., Bughin, J., Lund, S., Nottebohm, O., Poulter, D., Jauch, S. and Ramaswamy, S. (2014) *Global Flows in a Digital Age: How Trade, Finance, People, and Data Connect the World Economy*. McKinsey Global Institute. Available at: http://www.mckinsey.com/~/media/McKinsey/dotcom/Insights/Globalization/Global%20flows%20in%20a%20digital%20age/MGI_Global_flows_in_a_digial_age_Full_report.ashx (accessed September 2015).

Marriott, A. (2014) *A Dangerous Diversion: Will the IFC's Flagship Health PPP Bankrupt Lesotho's Ministry of Health?* Oxfam Briefing Note. CPAL (Consumers Protection Association [Lesotho])/Oxfam. Available at: http://policy-practice.oxfam. org.uk/publications/a-dangerous-diversion-will-the-ifcs-flagship-health-ppp-bankrupt-lesothos-minis-315183 (accessed August 2015).

Marx, K. (1858) *Grundrisse*. Notebook V – The Chapter on Capital. Available at: https://www.marxists.org/archive/marx/works/1857/grundrisse/ch10.htm (accessed September 2015).

Marx, K. (2010) *Capital*, Volume I. Marx/Engels Internet Archive (marxists.org). Available at: https://www.marxists.org/archive/marx/works/1867–c1/ (accessed April 2015) (first published 1867 (in German) Moscow: Progress Publishers).

McAlevey, J. (2015) 'Forging new class solidarities: organizing hospital workers'. *Socialist Register 2015*, 318–35.

McDermott, J.F.M. (2007) 'Producing labor-power'. *Science & Society* 71(3): 299–321. Available at: http://www.jstor.org/stable/40404421?seq=1#page_scan_tab_contents (accessed October 2015).

McKinsey & Company (undated) *Building India: Transforming the Nation's Logistics Infrastructure*. Available at: http://www.mckinsey.com/~/media/mckinsey%20offices/india/pdfs/building_india-transforming_the_nations_logistics_infrastructure.ashx (accessed September 2015).

McLean, B. (2007) 'Would you buy a bridge from this man?' *Fortune*, 2 October 2007. Available at: http://archive.fortune. com/2007/09/17/news/international/macquarie_infrastructure_funds.fortune/index.htm (accessed July 2015).

MCLI (Maputo Corridor Logistics Initiative) (undated) 'Maputo Development Corridor'. Available at: http://www.mcli.co.za/mcli-web/mdc/mdc.html (accessed September 2015).

Meek, J. (2012) 'Human revenue stream'. *LRB Blog*, 20 March 2012. Available at: http://www.lrb.co.uk/blog/2012/03/20/james-meek/human-revenue-stream/ (accessed July 2015).

Minns, R. and Sexton, S. (2006) *Too Many Grannies? Private Pensions, Corporate Welfare and Growing Insecurity*. Corner House Briefing 35. Sturminster Newton, Dorset: The Corner House. Available at: http://www.thecornerhouse.org.uk/resource/too-many-grannies (accessed August 2015).

Mitchell, T. (2002) *Rule of Experts: Egypt, Techno-Politics, Modernity*. Berkeley, CA: University of California Press.

Muschamp, H. (1994) 'Two for the roads: a vision of urban design'. *New York Times*, 13 February 1994. Available at: http://www.nytimes.com/1994/02/13/arts/architecture-view-two-for-the-roads-a-vision-of-urban-design.html (accessed July 2015).

Muzenda, D. (2009) *Increasing Private Investment in African Energy Infrastructure*. Background Paper, NEPAD-OECD Expert Africa Investment Initiative, Ministerial and Expert Roundtable, 11–12 November 2009. Available at: http://www.oecd.org/investment/investmentfordevelopment/43966848.pdf (accessed July 2015).

Nair, J. (2015) 'Indian urbanism and the terrain of the law'. *Economic and Political Weekly*, Vol. L, No. 36, 5 September 2015.

NDRC-PRC (National Development and Reform Commission – Peoples Republic of China) (2015) *Vision and Actions on Jointly Building Silk Road Economic Belt and 21st Century Maritime Silk Road*. National Development and Reform Commission. Available at: http://en.ndrc.gov.cn/newsrelease/201503/t20150330_669367.html (accessed September 2015).

Neilson, B. and Rossiter, N. (2014) 'Logistical worlds: territorial governance in Piraeus and the New Silk Road'. *Logistical Worlds – Infrastructure, Software, Labour* 1: 4–10. Available at: http://logisticalworlds.org/wp-content/uploads/2015/04/535_UWS_Logistical-Worlds-digest-2014–v10–WEB.pdf (accessed September 2015).

NEPAD (New Partnership for Africa's Development) (2008) *The RSDI & NEPAD Spatial Development Programme (SDP)*. Available at: http://www.mcli.co.za/mcli-web/events/2008/23jul2008/RSDI%20Presentation%20to%20UNECA%20ws%20July%202008.pdf (accessed September 2015).

Neruda, P. (2004) [1972] *The Captain's Verses*. New York: New Direction Books.

Netcare (2010) *Annual Report 2010: Participate with Passion*. Available at: http://www.netcareinvestor.co.za/reports/ar_2010/pdf/full.pdf (accessed August 2015).

Netcare (2014a) 'Lesotho health network public private partnership'. Media Statement, April 2014. Available at: http://business-humanrights.org/sites/default/files/media/documents/company_responses/netcare-response-re-lesotho-ppp-14–apr-2014.pdf (accessed August 2015).

Netcare (2014b) 'Analysis of shareholders at 30 September 2014'. Available at: http://www.netcareinvestor.co.za/share_shareholders.php (accessed August 2015).

Netcare (2015) 'Right to reply: "A study in financial extraction: Lesotho's National Referral Hospital"', response from Netcare and Tsepong to draft chapter, letter to the author, 9 December 2015. Available at: http://www.thecornerhouse.org.uk/sites/thecorner house.org.uk/files/Netcare%202015.pdf (accessed December 2015).

New World Academy (with the Kurdish Women's Movement) (2015) *Stateless Democracy*. New World Academy Reader No. 5. Available at: http://newworldsummit.eu/wp-content/uploads/2015/10/ NWA5–Stateless-Democracy1.pdf (accessed November 2015).

Noble, C. and Antonatos, L. (2014) 'What lies ahead'. *Infrastructure Investor Annual Review 2013*, *Infrastructure Investor*, March 2014.

Nostromo Research (2014) 'Pedra de Ferro – The Iron Stone (part 4)'. *Mines and Communities*, 30 September 2014. Available at: http:// www.minesandcommunities.org/article.php?a=12775 (accessed September 2015).

O'Carroll, S. (2013) *Mega Trends Driving Transport and Logistics in Sub-Saharan Africa: Trade Corridors Spur Regional Integration*. Frost & Sullivan. Available at: http://www.slideshare. net/FrostandSullivan/mega-trends-driving-transport-logistics- 6–2613?related=1 (accessed September 2015)

OECD (2011) *Pension Funds Investment in Infrastructure: A Survey*. Paris: OECD. Available at: http://www.oecd.org/futures/infra structureto2030/48634596.pdf (accessed July 2015).

OECD (2015a) *Low Interest Rates Threaten Solvency of Pension Funds and Insurers*. Paris: OECD. Available at: http://www.oecd. org/newsroom/low-interest-rates-threaten-solvency-of-pension- funds-and-insurers.htm (accessed August 2015).

OECD (2015b) *Mapping of Instruments and Incentives for Infrastructure Financing: A Taxonomy*, *OECD Report to G20 Finance Minister and Central Bank Governors*. Paris: OECD. Available at: http://www.oecd.org/daf/fin/private-pensions/ Mapping-Instruments-Incentives-Infrastructure-Financing- Taxonomy.pdf (accessed August 2015).

OECD (2015c) *Official Development Finance for Infrastructure: Support by Multilateral and Bilateral Development Partners*: OECD *Report to G20 Finance Ministers and Central Bank Governors*. Available at: https://g20.org/wp-content/uploads/2015/09/Official- Development-Finance-for-Infrastructure-Support-by-Multilateral- and-Bilateral-Development-Partners.pdf (accessed September 2015).

Owen, D. (2015) 'Lesson one from the Hinchingbrooke hospital scandal: beware the "mutual"'. *Guardian*, 19 January 2015.

Available at: http://www.theguardian.com/commentisfree/2015/jan/19/hinchingbrooke-hospital-scandal-mutual-privately-run (accessed June 2015).

Palmer, B.D. (2014) 'Reconsiderations of class: precariousness as proletarianization'. *Socialist Register 2014*, 40–60.

Pambazuka News (2015) 'Mozambican ministers must say "no" to resettlement of thousands in Nacala Corridor'. *Pambazuka News*, 14 May 2015. Available at: http://pambazuka.org/en/category/advocacy/94718 (accessed September 2015).

Paul, H. and Steinbrecher, R. (2013) *African Agricultural Growth Corridors and the New Alliance for Food Security and Nutrition: Who Benefits, Who Loses?* Econexus. Available at: http://www.econexus.info/sites/econexus/files/African_Agricultural_Growth_Corridors_&_New_Alliance_-_EcoNexus_June_2013.pdf (accessed September 2015).

PEI (Private Equity International) (2011) 'China LPs provided unprecedented liberties'. *Private Equity International*, 18 August 2011. Available at: http://www.privateequityinternational.com/article.aspx?article=62688 (accessed August 2015).

Peng, H.W. and Newell, G. (2007) *The Significance of Infrastructure in Investment Portfolios*. Paper presented at Pacific Rim Real Estate Society Conference, Freemantle, 21–24 January 2007. Available at: http://www.prres.net/papers/PENG_NEWELL_%20THE_SIGNIFICANCE_OF_INFRASTRUCTURE_IN_INVESTMENT_PORTFOLIOS.pdf (accessed August 2015).

PIDA (undated) *Financing PIDA Projects*. Available at: http://www.afdb.org/fileadmin/uploads/afdb/Documents/Generic-Documents/PIDA%20brief%20financing.pdf (accessed September 2015).

PIDA (2008) *Interconnecting, Integrating and Transforming a Continent*. Available at: http://www.afdb.org/fileadmin/uploads/afdb/Documents/Project-and-Operations/PIDA%20note%20English%20for%20web%200208.pdf (accessed September 2015).

Piketty, T. (2014) *Capital in the Twenty-First Century*. New Haven, CT: Harvard University Press.

Porto de Maputo (undated) 'Maputo Development Corridor region's most successful?' Available at: http://www.portmaputo.com/maputo-development-corridor-regions-most-successful/ (accessed September 2015).

Pozsar, Z., Adrian, T., Ashcraft, A. and Boesky, H. (2012) *Shadow Banking*. Staff Report No. 458. New York: Federal Reserve Bank of New York, July 2010, revised February 2012. Available at: http://www.newyorkfed.org/research/staff_reports/sr458.pdf (accessed July 2015).

Preqin (2015) 'The 2015 Preqin global infrastructure report'. *Infrastructure Spotlight* 7(1). Available at: https://www.preqin. com/docs/newsletters/inf/Preqin-Infrastructure-Spotlight-January-2015.pdf (accessed August 2015).

PWC (2013) *Health System Innovation in Lesotho.* Healthcare public-private partnerships series, No. 1. Available at: http://www. pwc.com/mx/es/industrias/archivo/2013–05–pwc-health-system-innovation.pdf (accessed August 2015).

Rallaband, G. (2013) 'Why high dwell times in African ports?' *Freight Into Africa,* 7 May 2013. Available at: http://www. freightintoafrica.com/article/why_high_dwell_times_in_african_ ports (accessed October 2015).

Republic of Indonesia (2011) *Masterplan for Acceleration and Expansion of Indonesia Economic Development.* Jakarta: Coordinating Ministry for Economic Affairs. Available at: http:// www.kemlu.go.id/rome/Documents/MP3EI_PDF.pdf (accessed September 2015).

Romei, V. (2013) 'Chart of the week: Brazil's bottlenecks'. *Financial Times,* 1 April 2013. Available at: http://blogs.ft.com/beyond-brics/2013/04/01/chart-of-the-week-brazils-bottlenecks/#axzz2Q w9gUJMt (accessed September 2015).

Romero, M.J. (2015) *What Lies Beneath? A Critical Assessment of PPPs and Their Impact on Sustainable Development.* Brussels: Eurodad. Available at: http://www.eurodad.org/files/ pdf/559da257b02ed.pdf (accessed July 2015).

Roodt, M.J. (2007) *Borderlands and Spatial Development Initiatives – The Impact of Regional Integration Initiatives in a Southern African Cross-Border Region: The Maputo Development Corridor.* Paper presented at the Inaugural Conference of the Institute for Social and Economic Studies. Available at: http:// www.iese.ac.mz/lib/publication/livros/South/IESE_South_3. BorSpa.pdf (accessed September 2015).

Rothballer, C. and Kaserer, C. (2012) 'The risk profile of infrastructure investments:challengingconventionalwisdom'.*JournalofStructured Finance* 18(2): 95–109. Available at: http://www.iijournals. com/doi/abs/10.3905/jsf.2012.18.2.095 (accessed July 2015).

Roy, A. (2014) *Capitalism: A Ghost Story.* London: Verso. Chapter 1 is available at: http://www.outlookindia.com/article/Capitalism-A-Ghost-Story/280234 (accessed April 2015).

RREEF (2011), *Listed Infrastructure: A Growing Landscape –*

Are You Ready? RREEF Infrastructure. Available at: http://realestate.deutscheawm.com/content/_media/Research_Listed_Infrastructure_A_Growing_Landscape_11_11.pdf (accessed July 2015).

Russell Investments (2014) *Index Industry Innovation Leads to Growing Adoption of ETFs Among Institutional Investors.* Available at: https://www.russell.com/documents/indexes/research/index-industry-innovation-leads-to-adoption-of-etfs.pdf (accessed July 2015).

S&P (2013a) *How To Unlock Long-Term Investment In EMEA Infrastructure.* Standard & Poor's *RatingsDirect.* Available at: http://www.engagedinvestor.co.uk/Journals/2013/10/22/d/p/m/How-To-Unlock-Long-Term-Investment-In-EMEA-Infrastructure_Oct2013.pdf (accessed August 2015).

S&P Capital IQ (2015) *Sector Disruptors: Infrastructure.* Market Intellect from Global Markets Intelligence, 8 May 2015. Available at: http://www.spcapitaliq.com/documents/our-thinking/research/sp-capitaliq-sector-disruptors-infrastructure.pdf (accessed May 2015).

Sangkoyo, H. (2015a) Personal communication.

Sangkoyo, H. (2015b) 'About commons, crisis and the inheritance of loss' in *Commoning as a Political Act: Conversations from Collevecchio.* Sturminster Newton, Dorset: The Corner House and Rome: Re:Common.

Sayer, A. (2015) *Why We Can't Afford the Rich.* Bristol: Policy Press.

Schmidt, I. (2011) 'Capital ideas: accumulation of capital – Rosa Luxemburg'. *Red Pepper,* May 2011. Available at: http://www.redpepper.org.uk/capital-ideas/ (accessed August 2015).

Schmidt, I. (2014) 'Rosa Luxemburg: economics for a new socialist project'. *New Politics* XV (1, Whole Number 57). Available at: http://newpol.org/print/content/rosa-luxemburg-economics-%E2%80%A8for-new-socialist-project (accessed August 2015).

Sewell, W. (1986) 'How classes are made: critical reflections on E. P. Thompson's theory of working-class formation'. Available at: http://deepblue.lib.umich.edu/bitstream/handle/2027.42/51104/336.pdf (accessed October 2015).

Shaoul, J., Stafford, A. and Stapleton, P. (2006) *Partnerships and the Role of the Big Four Accountancy Firms: Private Control Over Public Policy?* Paper presented at PRESOM seminar, Greenwich University, June 2006. Available at: http://www.raumplanung.tu-dortmund.de/irpud/presom/fileadmin/docs/presom/external/

WS_Greenwich_June_2006/Shaoul.pdf   (accessed   August 2014).

Shekhar, V. and Liow, J.C. (2014) 'Indonesia as a maritime power: Jokowi's vision, strategies, and obstacles ahead'. Washington, DC: Brookings Institution. Available at: http://www.brookings. edu/research/articles/2014/11/indonesia-maritime-liow-shekhar (accessed September 2015).

Sikka, P. (2012) 'The tax avoidance industry'. *Radical Statistics* 107: 15–30. Available at: http://www.radstats.org.uk/no107/Sikka107. pdf (accessed April 2015).

Silver, B. (2003) *Forces of Labor: Workers' Movements and Globalization since 1870*. New York: Cambridge University Press.

SME-CSMI (School of Mining Engineering and Centre for Sustainability in Mining and Industry) (2012) *Resources Corridors: Experiences, Economics and Engagement: A Typology of Sub-Saharan African Corridors*. Johannesburg: University of the Witwatersrand. Available at: http://www.eisourcebook.org/cms/ files/EISB%20Resources%20Corridors.pdf (accessed September 2015).

Stokes, J. (2015) 'China's road rules'. *Foreign Affairs*, 19 April 2015. Available at: https://www.foreignaffairs.com/articles/asia/2015– 04–19/chinas-road-rules (accessed September 2015).

Taibbi, M. (2010) 'The great American bubble machine'. *Rolling Stone*, 5 April 2010. Available at: http://www.rollingstone.com/ politics/news/the-great-american-bubble-machine-20100405 (accessed October 2015).

Tarr, J. (2005) 'The city and technology' in C. Pursell (ed.) *A Companion to American Technology*. Oxford: Blackwell Publishing, 97–112.

TATORT Kurdistan (2013) *Democratic Autonomy in North Kurdistan: The Council Movement, Gender Liberation and Ecology – in Practice*. Porsgrunn: New Compass Press.

Tawney, R.H. (1914) 'Poverty as an industrial problem'. Inaugural lecture, Ratan Tata Foundation. London: London School of Economics and Political Science. Cited in Sayer (2015, p. 29).

Thomson, A. (2014a) 'Star turn: interview with Tony Mallin of Star Capital'. *Infrastructure Investor*, 28 February 2014.

Thomson, A. (2014b) 'How times change'. *Infrastructure Investor Emerging Markets Handbook 2014*, June 2014.

Thomson, A. (2015) 'Nothing to fear: interview with Torbjorn Caesar, Actis'. Top keynote interviews 2015. *Infrastructure Investor*, 59–62, February–May 2015.

Thompson, E.P. (1991) *The Making of the English Working Class*. London: Penguin.

Timmins, N. and Giles, C. (2011) 'Private finance costs taxpayer £20bn'. *Financial Times*, 7 August 2011. Available at: http://www.ft.com/cms/s/0/65068d1c-bdd2–11e0–babc-00144feabdc0.html#axzz1YbE1rI9m (accessed August 2015).

Transport World Africa (2015) 'Mozambique coal: boom to bust to wait it out'. 28 July 2015. Available at: http://www.transportworld-africa.co.za/2015/07/28/mozambique-coal-boom-to-bust-to-wait-it-out/ (accessed September 2015).

UCU (University and College Union) (2012) *Public Service or Portfolio Investment? How Private Equity Funds are Taking Over Post-Secondary Education*. Available at: http://www.ucu.org.uk/media/pdf/0/l/ucu_psopi_oct12.pdf (accessed July 2015).

UNESC (United Nations Economic and Social Council) (2003) *Human Rights, Trade and Investment: Report of the High Commissioner for Human Rights*. New York: UN Economic and Social Council. Available at: http://www.unhchr.ch/Huridocda/Huridoca.nsf/e06a5300f90fa0238025668700518ca4/9b2b4fed82c88ee2c1256d7b002e47da/$FILE/G0314847.pdf (accessed August 2015).

Urban Land Institute/Ernst & Young (2013) *Infrastructure2013: Global Priorities, Global Insights*. Available at: http://www.ey.com/Publication/vwLUAssets/Infrastructure_2013/$FILE/Infrastructure_2013.pdf (accessed July 2015).

US Department of State (2013) '2013 Investment Climate Statement – Indonesia'. Bureau of Economic and Business Affairs, March 2013. Available at: http://www.state.gov/e/eb/rls/othr/ics/2013/204660.htm (accessed September 2015).

Vargas, M. (2012) 'IIRSA-COSIPLAN and European capital's responsibility' in Observatorio de la Deuda en la Globalización (ODG) and Transnational Institute (TNI) (eds) *Impunity Inc: Reflections on the 'Super-Rights' and 'Super-Powers' of Corporate Capital*, 86–105. Available at: http://odg.cat/MCA/ImpunityInc/docs/Impunity_Inc_Chapter_3.pdf (accessed September 2015).

Vargas, M. (2015) personal communication.

VCCSII (Vale Columbia Center on Sustainable International Investment) (2011) *Resource-Based Sustainable Development in the Lower Zambezi Basin*. Columbia University. Available at: http://ccsi.columbia.edu/files/2013/12/lowerzambezi.pdf (accessed September 2015).

Wagstyl, S. (2013) 'Rio: $3bn lost in Mozambique'. *Financial Times*, 17 January 2013. Available at: http://blogs.ft.com/

beyond-brics/2013/01/17/rio-3bn-lost-in-mozambique/ (accessed September 2015).

Weber, B. and Alfen, H. (2010) *Infrastructure as an Asset Class: Investment strategies, Project Finance and PPP.* Chichester: John Wiley and Sons.

WEF (2014a) 'Global competitiveness report: Brazil'. Available at: http://reports.weforum.org/global-competitiveness-report-2014–2015/economies/#economy=BRA (accessed September 2015).

WEF (2014b) 'Competiveness rankings'. Available at: http://reports.weforum.org/global-competitiveness-report-2014–2015/rankings/#indicatorId=GCI.A.02.01 (accessed September 2015).

Weng, L., Boedhihartono, A.K., Dirks, P.H.G.M., Dixon, J., Lubis, M.I. and Sayer, J.A. (2013) 'Mineral industries, growth corridors and agricultural development in Africa'. *Global Food Security* 2(3): 195–202. Available at: http://www.sciencedirect.com/science/article/pii/S2211912413000357 (accessed September 2015).

Whitfield, D. (2001) *Private Finance Initiative and Public Private Partnerships: What Future For Public Services?* Tralee, County Kerry: European Services Strategy Unit. Available at: http://www.european-services-strategy.org.uk/outsourcing-ppp-library/pfi-ppp/private-finance-initiative-and-public-private/what-future-pfi-ppp.doc (accessed August 2015).

Whitfield, D. (2014) *PPP Wealth Machine: UK and Global Trends in Trading Project Ownership.* European Services Strategy Unit Research Report No. 6. Tralee, County Kerry: European Services Strategy Unit. Available at: http://www.european-services-strategy.org.uk/publications/essu-research-reports/essu-research-report-no-6-ppp-wealth-machine-u/ppp-wealth-machine-final-full.pdf

Wilkinson, R. and Pickett, K. (2009) *The Spirit Level: Why More Equal Societies Almost Always Do Better.* London: Allen Lane.

Wilson, J., Bayón, M. and Diez, H. (2015a) *Postneoliberalism and Planetary Urbanization in the Ecuadorian Amazon.* CENEDET Working Paper No. 1. Centro Nacional de Estrategia Para El Derecho Al Territorio. Quito: Instituto de Altos Estudios Nacionales.

Wilson, J., Bayón, M. and Diez, H. (2015b) *Manta-Manaus: Interoceanic Fantasies and the Real of Planetary Urbanization.* CENEDET Working Paper No. 4. Centro Nacional de Estrategia Para El Derecho Al Territorio. Quito: Instituto de Altos Estudios Nacionales.

World Bank (2009) *Reshaping Economic Geography.* World

Development Report 2009. Washington, DC: World Bank. Part 1 available at: http://siteresources.worldbank.org/INTWDRS/Res ources/477365–1327525347307/8392086–1327528510568/ WDR09_bookweb_1.pdf; Part 2, 'Shaping Economic Geography', available at: http://siteresources.worldbank.org/INTWDRS/Res ources/477365–1327525347307/8392086–1327528510568/ WDR09_bookweb_2.pdf (accessed September 2015).

World Bank (2012) *Connecting to Compete: Trade Logistics in the Global Economy.* Washington, DC: World Bank. Available at: http://siteresources.worldbank.org/TRADE/Resources/239070– 1336654966193/LPI_2012_final.pdf#page=15 (accessed September 2015).

World Bank (2014a) *World Bank Group Support to Public–Private Partnerships: Lessons from Experience in Client Countries, FY02–12.* Washington, DC: Independent Evaluations Group, World Bank. Available at: https://openknowledge.worldbank.org/ bitstream/handle/10986/21309/936290WP0Box380ion000for0di sclosure.pdf?sequence=1 (accessed August 2015).

World Bank (2014b) *Running Water in India's Cities: A Review of Five Recent Public–Private Partnership Initiatives.* Washington, DC: Water and Sanitation Program, World Bank. Available at: https://www.wsp.org/sites/wsp.org/files/publications/Running-Water-in-India-Public-Private-Partnership-Initiatives.pdf (accessed August 2015).

World Bank (2014c) *Connecting to Compete: Trade Logistics in the Global Economy.* Washington, DC: World Bank. Available at: http:// d21a6b425f3bbaf58824–9ec594b5f9dc5376fe36450505ae1164. r12.cf2.rackcdn.com/LPI_Report_2014.pdf (accessed September 2015).

World Bank (2014d) 'Global Infrastructure Facility: About'. Washington, DC: World Bank. Available at: http://www.worldbank. org/en/programs/global-Infrastructure-facility#2 (accessed August 2015).

World Bank (2015a) *2014 Global PPI Update.* Washington, DC: Public–Private Partnership Group, World Bank. Available at: http://ppi.worldbank.org/~/media/GIAWB/PPI/Documents/Global-Notes/Global2014–PPI-Update.pdf (accessed August 2015).

World Bank (2015b) 'About'. Logistics Performance Index. Washington, DC: World Bank. Available at: http://lpi.worldbank. org/about (accessed September 2015).

World Bank (2015c) *Report on Recommended PPP Contractual Provisions.* Washington, DC: World Bank. Available at: http://ppp.

worldbank.org/public-private-partnership/sites/ppp.worldbank. org/files/documents/150808_wbg_report_on_recommended_ppp_ contractual_provisions.pdf (accessed September 2015).

World Bank/IMF/OECD (2015) *Capital Market Instruments to Mobilize Institutional Investors to Infrastructure and SME Financing in Emerging Market Economies: Report for the G20*. Available at: http://www.oecd.org/finance/financial-markets/WB-IMF-OECD-report-Capital-Markets-Instruments-for-Infrastructure-and-SME-Financing.pdf (accessed September 2015).

World Bank Institute (2012) *Best Practices in Public–Private Partnerships Financing in Latin America: The Role of Guarantees*. Washington, DC: World Bank. Available at: https:// einstitute.worldbank.org/ei/sites/default/files/Upload_Files/ BestPracticesPPPFinancingLatinAmericaguarantees.pdf (accessed August 2015).

WTO (World Trade Organization) (2011) 'Made in the World'. Available at: https://www.wto.org/english/res_e/statis_e/miwi_e/ miwi_e.htm (accessed September 2015).

WTO (2015) '"Made in the World" initiative news archives'. Available at: https://www.wto.org/english/news_e/archive_e/ miwi_arc_e.htm (accessed September 2015).

Xinhua (2015) 'China headlines: China pools strength on Belt and Road strategy'. *Xinhuanet*, 12 March 2015. Available at: http:// news.xinhuanet.com/english/2015–03/12/c_134062249.htm (accessed September 2015).

Zacune, J. (2006) *Globeleq: The Alternative Report*. London: War on Want. Available at: http://media.waronwant.org/sites/ default/files/Globeleq%20–%20The%20Alternative%20Report. pdf?_ga=1.50842412.466215235.1439632240 (accessed August 2014).

Zhang Zhao (2015) *China-Europe Rail Transport*. Sinotrans. Available at: http://fiata.com/fileadmin/user_upload/documents/ recent_views/Working_Group_UIC_FIATA/2_UIC-FIATA_ Vienna_23–24_April_2015_Presentation_Zhang_Zhao.pdf (accessed September 2015).

Zibechi, R. (2010) *Dispersing Power: Social Movements as Anti-State Forces*. Oakland, CA: AK Press.

Žižek, S. (1999) *The Ticklish Subject: The Absent Centre of Political Ontology*. London: Verso.